THE A TO Z

OF BEING UNDERSTOOD

make your voice heard and
your conversations count

Kay White

The A to Z of Being Understood

26 easy-to-apply principles to becoming a more savvy and influential communicator.

Find the ways and the words to engage and persuade people and make more lasting and profitable relationships, quickly and easily. Save time, money and energy as you go about your business.

ISBN 10: 0983169861
ISBN 13: 978-0-9831698-6-4

Published by: Expert Author Publishing
http://expertauthorpublishing.com

Canadian Address
1265 Charter Hill Drive
Coquitlam, BC, V3E 1P1
Phone: (604) 941-3041
Fax: (604) 944-7993

US Address
1300 Boblett Street
Unit A-218
Blaine, WA 98230
Phone: (866) 492-6623
Fax: (250) 493-6603

Cover design and layout: Pentacor book design, UK
Back cover photo: My Image Artist, USA

This book is dedicated to my parents,
Philip and Mary
and to my sister Claire.

They say you can choose your friends
but you can't choose your family.
I'd always choose you.

What other people say about this book

'In business as in life – to other people, you are what and how you communicate. *The A to Z of Being Understood* makes it easy and clear to understand *how* to be understood and why it's so important for you. Just using one of the principles can change your life – and Kay White gives you 26 to play with. Keep going back for another one and then work with it. Start to notice the difference in your results. Others will.'

Brian Tracy
Success Expert and best-selling author *The Psychology of Selling*

'Grab this book, read it and then use it. With *The A to Z of Being Understood* White teaches you her easy-to-use principles of how to interact, get results and inspire people as you go about your business. It'll make the difference that makes the difference for you, your career and your results, wherever you are in the world.'

John Assaraf
New York Times Bestselling Author, *The Answer* and *Having It All*

'I love this book! Every page is filled with a tid-bit of information you will want to burn into your memory.'

Lois P. Frankel, Ph.D.
Best-selling Author of *Nice Girls Don't Get the Corner Office* and *Nice Girls Just Don't Get It*

'*The A to Z of Being Understood* gives you the opportunity to get clear on what you can do to help others to really understand what you're about, what you want and how to get it! Pick a day, pick a place to start and work with Kay's tools, ideas and strategies. She grabs your attention from page one and walks you by the hand through the book.

As a successful business woman, I know just how key it is to be able to quickly connect and engage with the people around me and to make myself understood.'

Lisa Sasevich
Sales Conversion Expert and author of *The Invisible Close*

'Your income is directly tied to how well you can communicate. You'll never make more money than the level to which you can communicate with people. *The A to Z of Being Understood* has insights; tools and strategies laid out simply and logically for you and the information is brilliant, timeless and valuable. You make things better for yourself after you've read it.'

Bob Burnham
CEO of Expert Author Publishing
Author of *101 Reasons Why You Must Write a Book*

'Kay White has filled this easy-to-read and easy-to-implement guide to improving our communication skills with nuggets of information and insights based on her own experience, and her clients' that are truly life-changing. Never before have so many of us felt such a strong desire to be truly understood by our colleagues, friends and family – and never before have so many of us felt forced to give up that dream because of a lack of time and other pressures of modern life. Kay's brilliant new book, *The A to Z of Being Understood*, could not have arrived at a more ideal time.'

Tom Martin
President, Tom Martin Media, LLC

'My job as a trial lawyer is to get judges and ultimately juries to understand, and embrace my clients' case. When I need help in getting my message across, I reach into Kay White's magic toolbox, *The A to Z of Being Understood*, to find a strategy or an approach that will help construct a winning argument. When ticklish, tricky personnel and management matters land on my desk, Kay's calming and common sense advice brings clarity and most often – a ready way forward.'

Dennis Wade
Founding Partner, Wade Clark Mulcahy, Attorneys at Law

'If you think being understood is something that happens by lucky accident, well, you haven't read this book yet. Leaping across generations, cultural divides, and even the genders in a single bound, who says we can't turn the misery of misunderstanding into the glory of being understood, the first time! Thank goodness Kay White is here to make this simple, and clear – as crystal.'

Andrea J. Lee
CEO of The Wealthy Thought Leader and Author of *Pink Spoon Marketing*

Thank you, thank you, and thank you.

To all of you who believed in this book before I'd even started writing it.

Simon 'Snowy' White, my husband, my life-long case study and invisible hand-rail, thank you for giving me the space, support and encouragement to stop procrastinating and start writing. You always believe in what I do, often before I do so myself.

Special thanks go to my many mentors and friends Lisa Sasevich, Bob Burnham, Andrea J Lee, Susanna Dee, Pamela Mitchell, Tom Martin and Linda P Jones. You've inspired, supported, pushed and cajoled me and without your love and energy this book would still be a nice idea. To Steven Pressfield for writing *The War of Art*, the book that made me put down his and start to write my own.

Joan and Dave 'Ed' Morrison and Barry Shaw, thank you for your insights and edits and all your helpful suggestions and tweaks. Yvonne and Tracy at Pentacor, thank you for all your input too. This book has evolved, developed and been improved with all your beady eyes and helpful, objective suggestions.

Thank you to all the hundreds of clients along the way. You trust me as we work together, often on very sensitive issues, and then you share your results with me as you take on and use the principles and insights I offer you. You continually inspire and teach me, and many of you *star* in this book.

My thanks also go to all those people I've worked with and for during my own corporate career – Ted, Guy, Dom, James, Neil, Janet, Martin, Percy, Lorraine, David to name but a few. You taught me so much, even if it didn't *always* feel like it at the time, and you've shaped what I do (*and don't do*) now and how it helps people worldwide.

Finally and pertinently, thank you to Professors Gordon Rustin and Michael Seckl and all the team at the Oncology Department of Charing Cross Hospital, London. Without your work in the world, my work in the world wouldn't be possible. Simon King, you know the part you played.

It's been quite a ride and it's all part of the journey.

G is for Gratitude. Well, thank you.

Our journey from A to Z.
Pick a place to start.

A Place to Start

Travel is more than just A to Z; every part of the journey is connected.

Now there's a thought. To know where you're going, to be able to plan your journey, you have to know where you're starting. We're starting this journey together as a result of a random, powerful and one-off conversation I had on a plane.

The idea for this book came from a conversation whilst travelling at about 500 miles an hour, and 33,000 feet over the Atlantic.

I asked Craig, the wonderfully polite Purser on my flight from LA to London 'what do you think is the secret of being someone who finds it easy to get on with people?' I'd been watching him move around the cabin being helpful, polite and making people laugh. This was before I heard him speak. As he sorted out all my bits and pieces, showing me how to use things in and around my seat, I asked him the question.

He said, without hesitating 'courtesy, openness, respect – with a dash of fun.' His simple, straightforward answer got me thinking and I started jotting down other words I know to have a huge impact on connecting with people, being understood by people and with getting on with people.

As we start our journey from *The A to Z of Being Understood*, I promise I'll be courteous to you, open with you and respect you and your world. It is, after all, your world. Oh and let's also throw in a dash or more of fun (see J for Joker).

As my husband Snowy knows when he asks, 'what's for dinner?' there are always two choices. 'Take it or leave it.' It's up to you to decide how the tools and tips within these 26 insights; inspirations and ideas work for you. You too have the same two choices and, as with everything, you always do.

Whichever you choose, you're communicating and 'being understood' by others all the time, whether you think you are or not – even as you sit or stand reading this paragraph – so you may as well have a few more choices to play with as to *how* you're understood.

As Abraham Maslow said, 'if the only tool you've got in your toolbox is a hammer, you're going to treat everything you have like a nail.'

Writing this book is about you having more tools in your toolbox – everything from a feather duster, a magic wand, a tickling stick and a bow and arrow. You need more than one tool to work with, to get things done with, to engage and compel people. More than one tool to be understood.

It's such a magical thing to be in the world and be able to work confidently with, for and alongside others knowing that you are able to get to 'yes' or 'Yes!' or 'Ok then' without getting stuck, upset or – as Snowy says – 'bent out of shape'. Knowing these principles will make you more flexible, more comfortable and more confident. You'll be able to understand so much more about what goes on with other people as they're often misunderstood, frustrated, confused and you'll be able to avoid it happening to you. The more you use these principles, the more you'll want to and then you'll want to share them to help others too.

With this A to Z you can take one-a-day and work with that letter and its principles each day *or* go for the ramped-up dosage taking more than one, or all, of these 26 principles in one sitting.

Working with one a day, reading it the night before, again in the morning before you launch yourself into your day, that's my recommendation. You could share it with a colleague or your friend/partner and encourage each other. In less than a month – *26 days in fact* – these principles will become part of you. And, you can always come back for a refresher. There's a saying that 'you never step in a river the same place twice' – every time you pick the book up, you'll be reading it in a difference *place* in your life.

To know that you can take the short cut to being understood, to getting your message across to people more quickly and easily is my wish for you. How to be a savvier communicator – that's the *essence* of this book.

Stop flailing about hitting and missing like I did a while ago and as most other people are and always will. Take these principles, which I absolutely know, to my core, work and make a difference. Take them and help yourself – everywhere in your life.

I've written this book with professionals keen to advance their career and businesses in mind. As you read it you'll realise these principles will help you not just as you work – they'll help you to be understood everywhere and they're *particularly* effective as you go about your business.

Take them, practice them, discuss them, play with them and then notice the difference. Notice the difference in your confidence; your responses; others' responses to you; your relationships; your opportunities; your bank balance. They're all connected but then you know that too.

Thinking about it, this A to Z formula is a bit like a recipe for a casserole. One of those slow-cooking, nourishing meals that warm you up and sustains you. By combining all sorts of good ingredients into a pot, stirring it up and then simmering, something wonderful happens. As the ingredients fuse and infuse, a nourishing, warm and inviting meal is created. This is a casserole for you and, just like a casserole, you find the ingredients, measurements and flavours that work best for you. Then it becomes your recipe for success.

Inspirations for writing my book

'Life is a succession of lessons which must be lived to be understood.'
Helen Keller

'Nothing in life is to be feared, it is only to be understood. Now is the time to understand more, so that we may fear less.'
Marie Curie

'If you make yourself understood, you're always speaking well.'
Moliere

Attitude is a little thing that makes a BIG difference.

Winston Churchill

A *is for* Attitude

Your angle of approach

Insight for you

When I first read this, I had to read it twice.

> 'Your attitude, *not* your aptitude, will determine your altitude.'

The quote is by Zig Ziglar, American motivational speaker and author. I'd always thought attitude was something that described a person and their way of being. You've heard it so many times 'Oh, he's got a bad attitude' and 'You need to change your attitude', 'you've got the wrong attitude' – you can hear it.

Well, as a quote it's both motivational and thought-provoking but only if you *get* the real meaning of that word attitude. I didn't, I do now.

How far you go, how high you reach is more dependent on your attitude than how much you know, how qualified you are or how good you are at something. Your attitude is the key.

The word attitude comes from an aviation term – it's used day-to-day as a way of describing someone but when I asked Curt, a US naval pilot that question, he put it perfectly 'your attitude is the angle your nose meets the wind; it's your angle of approach' – the wind is a plane's resistance and the angle of approach of the plane (or 'your nose') directly affects the speed, the direction, the efficiency of the plane – or, for the purposes of our conversation together, you and your results.

So it's your angle of approach. Think about it. How you approach something; how you angle your nose to how you approach something.

When you think about a tricky situation, a fun plan you have, an interview, a meeting, a match – whatever, your attitude is going to determine your success more than anything else. More than that outfit you wear, the training you've done to prepare, the list of points you've made – more than all of those things.

Working with a client when I first started my business, I'd read an article on Attitude. The definition was laid out for me as I'm laying it out for you. I laid it out for her. At the time she was struggling with her team who she felt both fearful of and disconnected from. In our conversation I kept hearing that she found it 'impossible to get them to do things, their attitude is all wrong' and 'I want to scream at them one minute – and run for the hills the next.'

A bit cautiously – I was still trying it on for size myself – I told her that when you understand that your attitude to something, someone, a situation directly affects your personal results then it takes on a whole new 'angle of approach' that you have control over. 'You mean, I can angle my approach to what's going on at the moment and have it be completely different than if I hadn't?' 'Yes, and your angle of approach sounds like it is head on, win or lose, do or die, me versus them.'

Being able to connect and communicate who you are, what you're about, what you want and why you want it is the art of being understood. Of being the person able to get things done with, through and alongside people and it's what we want at a primal level. To be deeply connected to others – our families, our friends, clients, colleagues and our attitude has a direct result on how and if, that works for us.

Try these on for size.

The family party: You're off to a family 'do' and you're dreading it. You know it's a long way away, all sorts of aunties and uncles, cousins that you've always found dull and dreary will be there and the conversation will bore you. Oh, and there's a programme you love on TV and you'll miss the live result!

You arrive, the journey was dull but you're there now and here they all are. You go through the motions, smile (grimace at times) and make chit chat, looking at your watch from time to time and, when it's a time for you to 'exit stage left' you do so quickly, quietly saying 'oh, we must do this again' and make a dash for the car and disappear in a cloud of exhaust fumes.

A client change of plan: A client's just called – the plans have changed and instead of coming in an hour for the meeting you agreed, the one you're all prepared for – they're going to be with you tomorrow at 9am. Just exactly when you'd planned to be taking the car in for a service. 'Brilliant, bloody brilliant' you say as you put the phone down. You march into the kitchen, bang and crash about taking it out on the kettle, making a coffee clunking the cups about saying 'How could they? What a pain in the proverbial.'

My client's experience – your team seems to be disconnected, staying silent in meetings when you ask for feedback, looking at you as if you're speaking Swahili when you want information or input on something.

You say to other colleagues 'they're driving me nuts, their attitude is all wrong, it seems I'm the only one doing anything around here and when I tell them what I want all I seem to get for it is blank stares and shoulder shrugs.'

Well, fasten your seatbelts, let's change our angle of approach on these three real examples and find out what happens.

The family party: the angle of approach was one of painful, boring and something we 'have to' do.

What if your angle of approach was different? Instead it becomes 'a fact-finding mission to catch up with the family and have a few laughs, then be on my toes' or 'an opportunity to have some down-time on the journey and a few hours with people who've known me all my life and it's so rare we all get together.' Angling your approach this way changes how you get there, how you feel when you do and – of course – how you look (you might smile more than grimace) and actually enjoy yourself whilst you're there.

If you *choose* you can have fun at the get-together and still be on your toes in good time because you changed your attitude. *Your* angle of approaching it.

Client change of plan: So what about the client who called and changed plans? Your angle of approach could also be 'hmmm, more time to prepare and an early exit tonight. The car will have to wait, the client's more important.' It could also be 'OK, irritating and how does the car service work now? But actually this gives me some space to go through my emails and catch up with something else first. Heyho, these things happen. Move on.'

Simplistic I know, not always easy, I know too *but* by changing your attitude, you change – virtually on-the-spot – how you feel about it first and then, crucially, what you do next. You've changed the angle your nose meets the wind.

I know it's easy to say, 'yes but' and 'it's so bloody annoying and thoughtless' and 'why did they have to do it to me today of all days?' but how does this help you? Apart from the initial irritation, hanging on to that frustration and keeping that attitude of 'being done to' just slows you down and makes you tired and less productive. I still have to check in on myself and tweak my attitude to things – we're all work-in-progress after all.

People also notice a change in you when you choose and control your angle of approach. It's often a subtle change they notice 'hmm, she's not so fiery all the time' or 'wow, did you notice how he just let that one go' or 'how does he manage to get through those dull old meetings or networking events?' It's because of your attitude towards it.

Let's just go with my client's story and her angle of approaching her team and their meetings. She decided to think of them as part of her family – she didn't always like them but she loved them anyway. They had their ups and downs and so did she. Instead of telling them what she wanted them to do, I suggested she started asking them what was going on, what they were doing about it, what ideas they had, she did a survey for what they wanted their team meetings to be like and used the results to plan – virtually to the letter – the next team meeting.

Her results changed immediately. She was more relaxed – they all got the meetings they wanted and took some of the responsibility for them – and her attitude was 'hey, we're in this together and if I can change, so can you.' Oh, and by the way, she was promoted too.

Ideas for you to start working with today:

- Think of something or someone you're struggling with or something you're not looking forward to.

- Either jot down or say out aloud 'at the moment, my angle of approaching this situation or person is _____' and write/say what it is.

- Now, knowing what we know now, pick *at least* three other angles of approach you could take to the situation/thing and jot them down or say them out aloud – A more helpful angle of approaching this is:

1 _____

2 _____

3 _____

Pick one. By the way, write it down (it's more powerful if you do). Keep it with you – I suggest popping it into your purse/wallet/pocket. It may be that you combine your attitude to this with the three above and a more powerful fourth comes out.

Whatever happens know that you're choosing how you'll approach this – *how* your nose meets the wind – and just by doing this, I promise you, it will change *your* results, *your* experience of it *and*, crucially, how others notice and 'understand' you.

They are, after all, noticing how you are anyway – consciously or otherwise – so you may as well be understood and noticed in a way you want to be. You choose.

Inspirations for you:

'I discovered I always have choices and sometimes it's only a choice of attitude.'
Judith M. Knowlton

'Happiness is an attitude. We either make ourselves miserable, or happy and strong. The amount of work is the same.'
Francesca Reigler

'A happy person is not a person in a certain set of circumstances, but rather a person with a certain set of attitudes.'
Hugh Downs

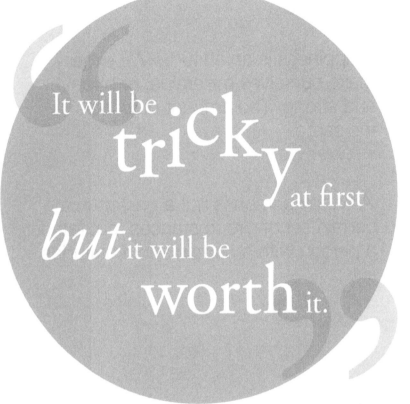

"It will be *tricky* at first *but* it will be **worth** it."

Kay White

B *is for* But

And how
it can trip
you up

Insight for you

When you're striving to be understood, to connect and persuade peo-ple it's often the little things that make a big difference. Really. When you learn the secret about the word 'but' it becomes the difference that often makes the difference for you in how people respond to you; how they remember you and what they'll say about you. Interested?

'But' must be treated like The Great Eraser. You hear it – *and wait for it* – countless times a day.

'That report was really great *but* the ending trailed off a bit' or 'That meeting was useful *but* it went on too long.' 'The people we met at the party were really friendly and we made some great contacts *but* the journey home was a nightmare.'

It's so powerful to know that *The Great Eraser* effectively erases from the mind of the listener what went before it, leaving what came after the 'but' as the part the listener most easily remembers (in fact it's often the *only* part they remember.)

'You made such a great case for the new product *but* we should have finished earlier' or 'You look great in that suit *but* your hem's coming down.' 'I really liked the way you made your point about the timing of the project *but* you could have brought out the benefits more.'

We've all been there haven't we? I can hear myself saying 'wait for it, here comes the but' and people will actually say it for you as you start off with the positive point and then they'll chime in with 'and here comes the but' don't they? By the way, 'however' is just 'but' in another outfit. Watch out and avoid 'however' too.

That's why I describe the word 'but' as a banana skin; a banana peel that can just literally trip you up when you least expect it. After all, you don't know what you don't know, do you? Or do you?

We often know intuitively that something's a bit off, that something could work better *but* until we understand it, it's a hit-and-miss affair. When we know, then we can change it and with practice, nail it. Change it and help others to do the same.

Why would you want to leave your listener, your reader, your friend with the negative part of your thinking? It just doesn't make sense to helping ease your way through conversations; meetings; reports; emails etc.

So, what do you do instead? A simple way is to flip it. Flip the way the sentence comes out. What comes before 'but' swaps places with what comes after it.

Put the negative first and follow it up with the positive. It gets the message out *but* the listener/reader is left with the positive part uppermost in their mind.

Try the phrases we've played with earlier – 'We should have finished earlier *but* you made such a great case for the new product.' 'Your hem's coming down and needs fixing *but* you look great in that suit.' 'You could have brought out the benefits of the project more *but* I really liked the way you made your point about the timing of it.'

Can you hear and feel the difference. Leaving the best bit hanging out in the listener's mind is a huge part of being remembered and noticed for being constructive, helpful and positive. All these are good ways for you to connect and engage people.

What's the point of putting out the positive first, laying it out for the listener or reader and then effectively erasing it with the 'but' placed after it? Flip it.

It takes some practice but then so did learning to ride a bike – a bit wobbly and uncomfortable at first. Learning to drive was, in my experience, the same. I had to do it very consciously at first – 'how will I ever remember to do all this?' and then gradually driving became second nature and I can do it whilst chatting or listening to the radio. Consciously placing 'but' in your sentence will be the same for you.

Put the even-better-if part out first, put your *and* after it and then finish with your positive part.

There's another way which is just as useful and it's another small, powerful word. You can use the word 'and' instead of 'but'.

Using the word 'and' is more like a bridge. I think of it as joining your sentence together versus breaking it up like the word 'but' does.

Having 'and' up your sleeve also helps when you've started your sentence in the traditional way *but* you can pop in the word 'and' instead.

Try our phrases from the beginning now with the bridge word 'and' instead – 'That report was really great *and* the ending trailed off a bit.' 'That meeting was useful *and* it went on too long.' 'The people we met at the party were really friendly, we made some great contacts *and* the journey home was a nightmare.'

It's powerful isn't it? It's simple too. You've kept the good part in *and* added the rest rather than erased the good bit with the word 'but'.

Clients say that just using this simple principle changes the way people respond to them. They notice there's a sort of sigh of relief when they use 'and' instead of 'but'. The same happens when you flip the sentence.

Try it on for size and then keep practicing it. You'll notice more and more how other people are being tripped up by their 'but' and leaving the listener hanging with the bad news and erasing the good news.

Watch out for *The Great Eraser.*

Ideas for you to start working with today:

- Notice where you put 'but' in your sentences. If you've started with the good stuff and can feel yourself about to say 'but', say 'and' instead.

- Start to think – just a nano-second before you speak – about *what* you want the listener to be left with. Put out the less positive part first, consciously do it. Then, with conviction, say the 'but' knowing that it will lessen the effect of the first bit and leave your listener with the good stuff. If you want to inspire and motivate people, this is key.

Inspirations for you:

It may seem a bit clunky and uncomfortable for you *but* it gets easier and then becomes natural.

The benefits will be noticeable virtually immediately *and* you'll have to practice. I still have to think about it sometimes *but* much less than I used to.

You probably knew this all along *but* now you know why.

Everything should be made as simple as possible, but not simpler.

Albert Einstein

C *is for* Clear

Be crystal,
when you
want to be

Insight for you

How many times have you sat in a meeting; been reading an article or listened to someone being interviewed on the TV or radio and wondered to yourself 'whatever are you saying – are you even talking English?.' I know I have – and still do.

> You and I both know that we're not really listening, we've tuned out and we're probably wondering what we're going to have for lunch?

One of the things I've noticed – and you'll have noticed it too – is that more and more there is a compulsion, for people to over-complicate, flounce up and confuse being seen to be clever for the price of being clear.

For the sake of clarity I shall call this type of language and approach 'gobbledegook'. It's an expression I use to cover those words and phrases we hear people use more and more like 'optimisation', 'strategic implementation', 'ambient capabilities'.

If you tune out, go a bit cross-eyed and get frustrated hearing these types of expressions well then so will your own listeners and readers.

Every client I've ever worked with, whenever we discuss this subject, without exception always says something like 'oh, I hate it' and 'hmm, I never really understand what that's all about', so avoid it.

You can *choose* if you use those words. From today, stop using them just because everyone else does and start translating them for people – and, crucially, for yourself. It will make a big difference for you right away.

'Gobbledegook' is dangerous – if you have a message to get across and it's wrapped up in words that people either tune out of or don't understand – then your message will be lost or diluted.

If you want to engage people with an idea or a way forward and they know it's important for them, when your message goes straight over their heads they'll resent you for it. We have to go off and find out from others 'what was going on in there?' or 'whatever was he/she saying?'. That's where Chinese Whispers start. Remember that game we used to play (and still do) where one person whispers something and the next tries to remember it and passes it on and so on? The message invariably changes by a word or two in the game. In meetings, it often changes even more dramatically because not only is the memory being tested for the actual words, the meaning of those words is being tested too.

Be clearer. Use the words that the 'gobbledegook' actually mean. You'll stand out for doing this because it's such a relief to hear real, day-to-day lingo as opposed to this trumped up, listen-to-how-clever-I-am sort of language.

Here's a great example from a client who sat in a meeting and, as he actually told me, 'I spent most of the meeting wondering what I was going to have for my lunch' but he decided to note some of the gobbledegook down and then translate it just to prove the point. Try this for size in case you needed convincing:

'May cause you to erroneously populate mandatory customer-authorised validation fields.'
You might put the information in incorrectly.

'If eligible we can validate the populated information to enable an accurate mandatory report to be submitted.'
We can make sure it's right.

'Automatic validation will provide you information on the validation and advise you of deficiencies if they exist on your mandatory reporting, this prevents ineligible reporting being submitted.'
Our system picks up mistakes, trust it.

'Dedicated customer service representatives are available to communicate and subsequently deliver the solution to the client.'
We have people here who will help.

'Present your issues to the client liaison development contact, and you will be afforded the opportunity, through a single source to satisfy your issues. We can do this through the most flexible and advanced technology reporting solution in the industry.'
Tell us your problem, we'll fix it because we have good people and a good system.

Which would you prefer to listen to? We both know that the listener of the chunks of clunky, overblown points above will, at best, get a rough idea of what the chap was trying to say and – at worst – have no idea at all. Nor care. He was trying to sell something and you can imagine, he was just making it harder for himself.

What's interesting to me is that trying to sound clever and smart actually does the opposite. Instead of being thought of as clever and smart, we actually think the person's a bit of an idiot, someone who's missed the point – *if they even had one.*

What I'm saying is work with what you have to – if a project's called 'Operation Strategic Implementation' then you can add 'by that I mean' or 'in other words'. It's a subtle way of working with the words and helping both yourself and the person on the receiving end. If you can choose from the start 'use the straightforward version.

'KISS' – Keep It Simple and Straightforward. Why wouldn't you?

Ideas for you to start working with today:

Being understood is all about just that. Make it easier for yourself and others to connect with you.

Here are some tips for you to translate what's being said. You can ask these questions to yourself and then ask your colleagues, your boss, your team, your clients when you're trying to get to the core of what's being said. I do and they work.

One way: Ask 'If I were 5 years old, what's going on?' If you haven't got a 5 year old in your life, then I can guarantee you *were* one. A 5 year-old speaks plain, straightforward English.

I asked a client once 'Uncle David, I'm 5 years old and I don't understand what you've been saying about Key Performance Indicators and reward optimisations. What do you mean?' He looked at me for a second as if I'd lost the plot and then, after some head-scratching and a bit of giggling, he said 'some naughty people are playing some nasty games because they think we're going to take their toys away?' Aha, now we knew *both* what was going on.

So ask that question 'If I were 5 years old, what's going on?' Go on, I dare you to. It's actually a relief for people to cut through the gobbledegook.

Another way: I call this 'Pillow Talk'. What would you say to your wife/husband/partner if you were in bed chatting about this subject?

I doubt you'd lie there and look over and say, 'The consultants recommend compatible relative options, we must expedite immediately.' I know if I said that my husband would roll over immediately and start snoring. He'd also wonder if he'd married a corporate clone.

You're more likely to say 'well, the people we had in to look at things gave us a few choices that seem to fit. We've got to decide what to do next.'

Again, you can ask this question to yourself as you're putting a report together or preparing a presentation or ask your colleagues. In a meeting it can be so helpful if someone actually says 'what are we *really* talking about here?' or 'what would you say to your partner about this if you were chatting about it in bed?'

Go on, use this question, just like the 'If I were a 5 year old' one. Use it on yourself, your colleagues and – trust me – to prove a point, tell your partner how much it helps you using them as a person to imagine talking to in meetings, reports etc. They'll be pleased to know you think about them like that – aha – a win/win.

Yes, I know a lot of people would say they've got better things to do in bed – sleep being one of them – but you get my point. It's another way to translate clunky, overblown expressions.

If you're confused about what's going on, what hope have your audience or readers got?

Inspirations for you:

'I know that you believe you understand what you think I said, but I'm not sure you realize that what you heard is not what I meant.'
Robert McCloskey

'The ability to simplify means to eliminate the unnecessary so that the necessary may speak.'
Hans Hofmann

'They may forget what you said, but they will never forget how you made them feel.'
Carl W. Buechner

"He who dares not offend cannot be honest."

Thomas Paine

 D *is for* Direct

How and why it's good to be

Insight for you

It's important to be able to be direct. There are times when it's crucial to be direct. It helps people – you included. There you are, I'm being direct with you. It's got your attention, you know what I'm saying and – assuming we're on this journey from A to Z because you're interested in being better understood – is a key piece to being understood.

We'll start with the 'Why' of being direct first. I'll be direct with you.

So many people struggle with saying what has to be said. They 'beat about the bush' as we say, chatting about everything else but what they actually *want* to say. We can feel they're struggling, they can, and the longer it goes on the harder it is for them to say what *has* to be said.

If you think about it, more often than not, when someone is direct with you, it's actually a relief. You know and understand what they're saying, you're able to decide whether to take the information or their opinion on board and you can keep moving.

I believe the struggle with being direct is two-fold. Firstly it stems from fear. It's a primal fear of rejection at the root of being unable to be direct. Putting an opinion or instruction out and either hurting someone's feelings or being seen to be 'wrong' is scary.

The struggle is both about fear and it's about thinking that you have to please everyone all the time. The trick is to be able to respect the other person's position or point of view *and* still be able to put across your own.

'This is going off-track. We have to get those expenses down otherwise all the budgets will be blown.' This direct opinion has given us everything we need to understand that something's going wrong, there's a direct action required and the consequence is laid out for us if we leave things. We may not like the message, it may not be strictly true but at least we know what the other person is thinking.

You can imagine that this, direct opinion could have gone like this and, in many meetings I've been in has 'Well, we've got to be careful to understand how exactly the numbers are all adding up at the moment. We've said it before and it's time to say it again, that, if we aren't very strict with ourselves and what we're spending then the whole project could be jeopardised and then we might all be at risk of being told the budgets have been blown and then who knows where we'll be?' Phew, we got there. It was painful and 'clunky' to get there and – *if* they held our attention on to the end of it – the importance of the message has been severely diluted.

Can you see in the second version that as well as diluting the message, there is also a real danger of both confusing and, crucially, boring your audience? Be it a listener, a reader, a crowd – your audience is the person or people you're communicating with. You want their attention not their resentment or doubt. Personally, I resent spending my precious time listening to or being made to read something that's rambling, jumbled and woolly. My brain has enough stuff vying for attention and so does yours. It's a relief when someone tells you what's what.

A simple example of this is when you open a website. If there's a great chunk of text and you find yourself scanning to get what it's about, chances are you'll skip it or you'll close it and go to another site. Any website designer will tell you that people skim read, filtering all the time and that to grab them by the eyeballs, words must be straightforward, punctuated and brief. When you want to get a message across to people, think about how you surf the internet. The principle is the same. Clear, brief, punctuated, pause.

It's OK to be direct. It's more than OK in fact. Most people will love you for it. They actually want your opinion and they can then choose whether they take your opinion on, or not. Just as you can choose whether you take someone else's opinion too. You choose.

Getting older and, we hope, wiser, we realise when someone tells us how it is (or in reality, how they *think* it is) we grasp what's being said because it's separated from the 'blah' as I call it. They save us time translating and pulling the message out of the 'blah'. Just like a good website designer does.

Try another one on for size. 'That colour is a bit drab on you. You look lovely in blue. It brings out the colour of your eyes.'

Again, we may not *like* the information we've been given but at least the message is clear. As far as that person is concerned, we could look better in another colour. We now have a choice, act on it or ignore it. At least we know what they're saying.

Instead of writing out for you all the long-winded ways that phrase could have been said including the 'well you could' and 'it's only my view but' (notice the *B for but*) etc, I know you get the message. It's OK, in fact I believe it's crucial, to have an opinion. Put it out there for people and then pause.

Now let's think about the 'how' of being direct.

There are many ways to be direct. Some more effective than others.

- When speaking, you've been around long enough to know already that your tone of voice plays a big part in being listened to and taken notice of.

- If you express your direct response in a flat, monosyllabic tone then your audience again has to struggle with getting past your tone (see T is for Tone for much more detail on this).
  Again, if your tone goes up at the end so that your statement becomes a question, this is less effective – and surprisingly irritating too. 'I think we should go on Friday' becomes 'I think we should go on Friday?' Turning a statement into a question puts doubt in the mind of the listener.

- If and when you smile. Smiling actually relaxes you. There's a chemical response inside of us to smiling. Studies show that smiling releases endorphins, natural painkillers, and serotonin. Together these make us feel good. Interestingly, your brain can't tell if you're smiling naturally or if you're making yourself smile. The reaction is the same. So allow yourself to smile – your message is still clear *and* it's easier to talk with a smile.

There's a formula to being more usefully direct.

- Give your Opinion + a Reason + offer a Solution. 'That colour is a bit drab on you. (opinion) You look lovely in blue (solution). It brings out the colour of your eyes (reason).' How about this one – 'This is going off-track. (opinion) We have to get those expenses down (solution) otherwise all the budgets will be blown (reason).'

- It's less about the order you express yourself and more about having the components in there. Opinion + Reason + Solution = Usefully Direct.

Ideas for you to start working with today:

- When someone asks you for your opinion, give it. They've asked you and even if they don't like it when you give it, they asked you for it so respect them and tell them what you think. 'What do you think?' or 'What's your take on this?' Tell them.

- Use the formula: Opinion + Reason + Solution = Usefully Direct.

- Keep your sentences short and clear. You can do it. Remember the 'C for Clear' ideas – 'If I were 5 years old, what's going on?' and the 'Pillow Talk' tips help you do this.

- Remember, if your intention of being direct is to help someone understand (or be understood) then your intention is true. As you become more comfortable being direct, you help people understand your opinion *and* that your opinion counts. There, I've been direct with you.

Inspirations for you:

'A gentleman gives direct answers, especially to controversial questions. Being direct, however, is not that same thing as being rude'

John Bridges

'Any intelligent fool can make things bigger, more complex, and more violent. It takes a touch of genius – and a lot of courage – to move in the opposite direction.'

E. F. Schumacher

'When you want something, start with the direct approach. That is, go straight to the source and ask for what you want. You will be surprised at how often you get it.'

John T Reed

"Colours, like features, follow the changes of the emotions."

Pablo Picasso

E *is for* Emotion

Oh, the 'touchy, feely' stuff

Insight for you

It was the start of a meeting with a potential new client. As we sat discussing what was going on with his team, and why some of the key people were avoiding communicating with each other, let's call him John, said something along the lines of 'well, we've brought you in because it's probably all about the touchy, feely stuff and Kay, I don't do that.'

'You don't do that?' I said, risking, I suppose, being shown the door, 'You don't do that? Everyone does that John, everyone does that all the time, it's what it's all about.' How's that for direct? How's that for an opinion? It's mine and I know it to my core. Two choices – as ever – take it or leave it but it's true.

When someone explained to me once that emotion can be defined as 'energy-in-motion' it took on new meaning, one that really makes sense and, to all those 'oh, I avoid the touchy-feely stuff' out there, think about emotion like this – it's 'energy-in-motion'. Your energy, at any given moment, can change to another energy and you behave differently. Something else happens and, depending how you decide to react to it, (notice I said 'how you decide') then your emotion changes again.

To help us both be clear, throughout this principle, I'll put the emotion in (*italics and in brackets*). As you go through your day, start noticing your own emotions and, crucially others' (*they're on display, you just have to notice them*). As you become more and more aware that emotion is driving everything, and everyone, you'll be able to understand so much more about other people and so much more about yourself.

Here's a typical scenario that plays out every day, for someone, somewhere.

Rushing to a meeting to avoid being late (*excitement, fear*) you arrive just as the meeting's starting (*anxiety, embarrassment*). As you grab a coffee and your seat (*relief, anticipation*) you're asked a question (*surprise and fear again*). Someone else chimes in to help you (*relief and surprise*) and you also gather your thoughts and add your opinion (*relief and anticipation*). The meeting carries on and you notice yourself relaxing (*contentment and trust*) and you're asked to be involved in a new project (*surprise and joy*). You know it'll be hard work with a lot riding on it and you say 'yes, great' (*anticipation, fear, joy*) and you all agree to meet again in two weeks to update everyone (*anticipation, trust, anxiety*). Off you go to your desk and pick up the phone to tell your partner about this opportunity (*excitement and surprise mixed with anxiety*).

Can you 'feel' just from reading the above, how much energy-in-motion is going on, just in that meeting?

We are constantly shifting and changing gear with our emotions and the more we understand about how they affect us, and those around us, the more we can start to take notice of where we are in our emotional journey.

That's why when John, above, said 'oh, the touchy feely stuff' I responded like I did (*surprise and irritation*) to his comment (*fear and frustration*).

We're *all* in an emotional state, all of the time. The trick is to notice *which* emotional state we're in – relaxed, excited, angry, frustrated, sad, happy – and to know that we are moving in and out of these states all the time. The trick is to decide and find which state is the most helpful, appropriate, resourceful for us to be in given what's going on around us.

The sun came out for me when I really started to notice my own emotions and recognised how, depending on how I think about something and respond to something either happening or not happening, then my emotional state changed. We move from one 'state' to another and we are *driven* by our emotions.

Daniel Goleman's *Emotional Intelligence* is a ground-breaking book which is, in my opinion, the equivalent of a User's Guide to understanding our brain and how it drives our emotions. When I say 'it drives our emotions', we both understand this really means '*we* drive our emotions' – we have the steering wheel. That's where John was struggling; recognizing and taking responsibility for his and to a large extent, his team's emotions.

Let's look to some of the experts to help in understanding and identifying emotions and then we can work more closely together to understand our own.

A good place to start is Robert Plutchick's *Wheel of Emotions*. Plutchik's psycho-evolutionary theory of emotion is considered one of the most influential classification approaches for general emotional responses. He considered there to be eight primary emotions: anger, fear, sadness, disgust, surprise, anticipation, trust and joy.

Robert Plutchick's theory of emotion is a great example of KISS in practice. His *Wheel of Emotions* is simple and straightforward and consists of:
Eight basic emotions with their basic opposites plus
Eight advanced emotions each composed of two of the basic ones.

We're going to pull out the eight basic ones here and you'll easily be able to find out more about the advanced ones, but this is a great place to start.

These give us the ingredients for our emotional recipes.

Basic emotion	Basic opposite
Joy	Sadness
Trust	Disgust
Fear	Anger
Surprise	Anticipation
Sadness	Joy
Disgust	Trust
Anger	Fear
Anticipation	Surprise

Once we recognise that *we're all* emotional beings – yes, even you John – and that *we* are responsible for our own emotional state, we then understand we're all energy-in-motion – all the time.

We move in and out of emotional states and on to other ones all day, every day. People say 'oh, he was in a right state about that.' Well, he was in a state, an emotional state. The trick is, which one and how well did it work for him to be in that state?

Let's explore another example. Remember, we all respond differently, but for our purposes I'm mapping this out as I think about it and combining the emotions set out for us above. It'll tell you something about my own emotions and how I 'feel' it could play out.

You're on your way to the cinema to meet friends (*anticipation, joy*). You find a great parking space (*surprise, joy*) and then your friends ring to say they're stuck in traffic but they should be there before the film starts (*surprise, anger*). You go to buy the tickets and start to think about all the times they've been late before (*anger, sadness*).

The phone rings again and your friends are close but now they can't find a parking space (*joy, anticipation*). You ask what time the adverts finish and the film starts and you find out there's ten minutes to go (*anticipation, fear*). Your friends rush through the door (*joy, surprise, anticipation*), you go inside together, find your seats and the film starts (*anticipation, joy*) – and then – depending on the film and how you react to it, *fear, sadness, joy, surprise* because that's what film-makers are constantly aware of and searching for, ways to evoke emotion in their audiences.

The trick for our purposes on our journey of working with and alongside people is to recognise and understand *which* emotion we're experiencing at any given time and ask ourselves 'Does this emotional state work best for me in the circumstances?' Remember we have the steering wheel.

Then, as you prepare emails, presentations, reports, as you go to meetings and speak up, notice your emotions, be more aware of others' emotions and how you are *allowing* them to affect you. If someone is happy, laughing, positive, helpful, then they can – if you choose – evoke joy in you. You can easily imagine the *opposite* too, but now you know it's because you're *allowing* them to evoke that emotion in you.

The knack is to be *aware* first and then you'll find that you will have to ditch those phrases '*oh he makes me* so angry' and '*she always makes me* feel better' because you know now that you're responding to their emotional states and allowing them to 'make' you change your own (*surprise, fear, anticipation*). Who's driving the bus? Who's got the steering wheel?

Just as it's important to notice how you allow others to make you feel, it's important to know, as far as being understood yourself that people won't always remember what you *said*, but they'll *always* remember how you made them *feel*. Aha.

Ideas for you to start working with today:

- Notice – really notice – how you're feeling. Try to tell yourself which emotion you're feeling as you go through your day. Does this emotion serve you best for what's going on?

- Knowing now how we 'drive' our own emotions, moment by moment, start to drive your own more. Decide, 'am I going to allow this situation to make me feel angry?' or 'if I were only to feel happy about this, what would I have to think about instead?'

- Now you're noticing what you notice about your own emotions, it's time to notice others'. Notice how they're reacting or responding to things and – crucially here – notice how they make you feel (or how *you allow them to make you feel*). Towards the end of your day today, run through this chapter again and think about your day. Which emotions came up for you and what was happening when they did?

Inspirations for you:

'Let's not forget that the little emotions are the great captains of our lives and we obey them without realising it.'
Vincent Van Gogh

'When dealing with people, remember you are not dealing with creatures of logic, but creatures of emotion.'
Dale Carnegie

'Feelings are much like waves, we can't stop them from coming but we can choose which one to surf.'
Jonatan Mårtensson

"

FEEDBACK
is the
breakfast
of
champions.

"

Ken Blanchard

is for Feedback

www.ebi.ok

Insight for you

What? www.ebi.ok? Go to that web address and there's nothing there. It's made up for you to be able to remember a simple formula for giving others feedback and – importantly – for you to be able to ask others for feedback yourself.

It's a great word 'feedback'. The dictionary on my trusty Mac defines it as

'Information about reactions to a product, a person's performance of a task etc. Used as a basis for improvement.'

Ask for it, offer it, be prepared to think about the feedback you get to really help you. There's a lot going on as we go about our business, other people notice things we can't either see or understand. That's OK. Let's grab this information, be open to it and use it to improve ourselves. Use it to move forward.

Asking for feedback and taking it on is a huge part of how to get better at what you're doing and understanding how people think about you. Also, asking a person for feedback is a compliment – it tells them you trust them, that you value their opinion. By asking some-one for their feedback, you're asking them to think about you and notice what you're doing and how you're doing it.

Remember the nuggets from the dictionary definitions and feedback is defined as 'Used as a basis for improvement' and 'information'. Think about how you learned to walk, to ride your bike, to read, to write.

If you were lucky enough to have people around you who encouraged you, told you how to pronounce words so you were saying them correctly; told you how to balance as you were wobbling about on your first bike and explained the difference between what you were doing and what you needed to do to be able to balance – they were giving you feedback; giving you information and helping you to improve.

What they weren't doing – again, if you were lucky enough to have supportive mentors around you – was telling you as you were learning how to walk 'oh dear, you've fallen over, you're hopeless and I wouldn't bother' or 'crikey, can't you ride that bike yet? You've had it a week now. Give it to someone else, you'll never be able to do it.'

What they also weren't doing was telling you 'oh, you're so brilliant. That's just great, keep practising.' All very lovely and not very useful. Giving and receiving feedback is much more than that. It's about what's working and what can be done to improve it, to make it even better. That, for me, is feedback in a nutshell.

These sorts of examples of a person's performance, our performance, are when we really notice how crucial feedback is. It's how we learn, grow and develop and feedback comes from a positive place and a positive attitude. A positive 'angle of approach'.

The essence of feedback is acknowledging what's working and giving information as a basis of improvement about what could make it work even better.

Let's use our wobbling first bike ride as an example. 'That's right, hold on to the garden table, sit up and get your balance first; now look ahead to where you're going and – gently – pedal and let go. I'll run alongside you.' Then, after trying this, 'now that was great and much better than before, your balance seemed better and if you let go of the table sooner, your balance will be spot on. Try it again now, this time letting go of the table as soon as you start to pedal. OK?'

You get the idea. It's about telling you what's working, what you noticed could be better to enable you to improve and suggesting ways to do that.

Here's the formula again – **www.ebi.ok**.

What Went Well, Even Better If. OK?

It's really handy to have this in your mind. You can sum up a meeting, a proposed idea, an appraisal, a meal by using www.ebi.ok. All in the spirit of wanting the person, or the situation, to improve.

www: 'That report is really great. It's punchy, well laid out and I can see where you're going with it.

ebi: It will help it flow if you put a few bullet points in and highlight the titles.

ok: Does that make sense?'

It's so simple and effective. Laying out what's working or what went well first. Remembering here how 'but' can trip you up, you pause. Instead you say 'what will make it even better is' or 'it'll be even better if'. Can you hear – and feel – the subtle effect of 'even better'. It tells us that *it's already good* and what I'm about to offer you will make it *better.*

This formula helps us just as much in our social lives as it does in our professional ones. Being open to giving and, crucially, receiving feedback with the intention of helping someone – or being helped – to improve will help you to stay a life-long-learner. Noticing what's going on, thinking about what either you or the person wants to achieve, offering your feedback, it's a gift. It's a gift to have feedback and treating it as such, we say 'thank you' for it.

A quick example of this in action for you. We were having dinner in a restaurant and the manager was moving from table to table asking diners how their meals were, if everything was OK for them. She was stunning. She looked Italian with long, thick dark hair and a beaming smile. Snowy and I both agreed she really stood out and was very attractive (us Brits looking very un-Italian). Snowy commented to me along the lines of 'shame she's got those dreadful trousers on, they make her look so much bigger than she is.' Hmm.

When she came to our table and we'd exchanged pleasantries and I decided to try the **www.ebi.ok** formula. Smiling and nodding to her I said 'You look so glamorous with your exotic Italian looks' (www) she smiled and thanked me 'and I know that if it was me I'd really want to know that those trousers you're wearing really don't do you justice. They definitely make you look bigger than you are and who wants that? (ebi). I thought you'd want to know because I know I would (ok).' She laughed and immediately said 'thank you – do you know, I wondered that myself. I grabbed them to put on this evening and haven't felt right in them. Thank you for telling me. They're going to the charity shop tomorrow morning.'

Snowy was somewhat squirming in his seat, wondering if we were going to have a jug of water thrown over us. We didn't. She was pleased and interestingly knew it, deep down. I felt better that I hadn't said it behind her back, I'd said it to her face but in a way that was helpful and positive. She asked us what we'd like to drink 'on the house'. Enough said.

Ideas for you to start working with today:

- Jot down **www.ebi.ok** in your notebook or on a Post-it Note and pop it on your desk.

- Know that your intention is to help others to improve. If you spot something or someone who's doing a great job with something *and* (if you've read the chapter about B for But you already know that you're avoiding 'but' – *The Great Eraser)* you know it could be 'even better', then tell them using the formula. Start with the www, lead into the ebi with something like 'and you know, if you do X as well then it will be even better. What do you think?'

- Be open to it yourself. Be open to asking for feedback i.e. how can I improve on this or be even better? Ask for feedback. The most effective way to do this is to ask questions. If you ask someone 'is this OK?' they may just say 'yes' or 'no'. If you ask them 'now, what do you think of X, Y, Z? I'm open to feedback and genuinely want to know what you think.' Then wait. You've asked them so let them think about it and give you their thoughts. Then ask them 'and what do you think I could do to make it even better?' You're telling them – via your question – that you think it's good, it's getting there, you just want them to tell you how to make it *even* better.

- Enjoy having the 'breakfast of champions' every day. If everyone just tells you 'you're great' all the time, it's far less useful than if they tell you for example 'you're great and if you just slowed down a bit sometimes etc' it gives you something to work with, something to work on to improve. It's a gift.

- If you've received great service from someone or from an organisation – or less than great service – try using this formula just to let them know about it. People are so much more receptive to improving when they receive the suggestion with 'what went well' or what they're doing well *first*.

Inspirations for you:

'Everyone needs feedback, and it's a heck of a lot cheaper than paying a trainer.'
Doug Lowenstein

'You need to know about customer feedback that says things should be better.'
Bill Gates

'What is the shortest word in the English language that contains the letters: abcdef? Answer: feedback. Don't forget that feedback is one of the essential elements of good communication.'
Unknown

"

Silent gratitude isn't much use to **anyone**.

Gladys Browyn Stern

G *is for* Gratitude

Well, thank you

Insight for you

It's such a small thing to say 'thank you'. It costs you absolutely nothing and it makes a *huge* difference to how you are understood and remembered by people. Saying 'thank you' also changes how you feel about yourself.

Most people – if they're lucky, in my opinion – from when they were a small child were taught that 'thank you' is what you say as soon as you're given something – in my case I would have something taken back from me until I said 'thank you' – so it was pretty simple. As soon as someone gives you something or does something for you, be grateful. Say 'thank you'. I constantly wonder why don't we say 'thank you' more often?

To be remembered and recognised in a way that works for us, we need to make people *feel* a certain way – remember, E for Emotion, the touchy-feely stuff? Well here's an easy, effective *and* natural way to make people *feel* that you appreciate them. Say 'thank you' more. More than you probably do at the moment.

Once I started noticing this and how and where I could be more thankful, more appreciative of what people do and are doing, not just *for* me but *around* me, there were and still are loads more opportunities to say 'thank you'.

'Thank you for your help', 'thanks for telling me that', 'thank you for letting me know', 'thank you for just being around', 'thank you for thinking of me'.

The two words – thank you – are defined in the dictionary as 'a polite expression used when acknowledging a gift, service or compliment or accepting or refusing an offer'. Simple.

Now please know that by including this principle, I'm only suggesting that you say thank you *more* – not that you don't say it already. Start to think about being grateful more and, when you do, instead of just noticing that you're grateful, *saying* it more.

'Thank you' is an expression of gratitude. Being grateful is now recognised as being a positive emotional state. So much so that the Positive Psychology movement is both recognised and respected by the psychology profession – the essence being that the more we show 'an attitude of gratitude', the more positive we feel about what's going on. A win/win then.

Attitude, as we know from the beginning of this book is 'the angle your nose meets the wind'. Angle your nose to meet the wind by being grateful and looking for ways and chances to thank people. Instead of the attitude I hear so many people mutter 'well, they're just doing their job' or 'I was so pleased with how they did that' and when I ask the person 'did you tell them you're pleased?' they invariably say the person was either doing what they were supposed to or they just assumed the person knew they were pleased.

No more 'assuming' with thanks and, as corny a phrase as it is, it's still true – 'To assume makes an Ass out of You and Me' – not wanting to *assume* you'd heard it before I've put it here for you too.

You'll make someone's day as you do and, it has a great knock on effect – you feel better too.

Ideas for you to start working with today:

- Decide to notice and be on the look out for opportunities to say 'thank you' more today. Clearly I mean for you to *mean* that you're grateful as opposed to just *saying* you are.

- Start your emails off with 'Thank you for' as an example. If you're running a meeting, thank the participants for being there, for their time etc. Even if 'it's their job to be there' *thank* them for being there. You can't do it on your own and without them, there would be nothing to talk about anyway.

- If you're responding to someone who has irritated you or said something – especially in an email – that's annoyed you, try saying 'thank you' first. Thank them for giving you the information, for giving you their thoughts, for pointing out what they did. Whatever it is, thank them for it *first*.

- When someone helps you today – they will, and they do all the time – for example; by opening or holding the door for you, by serving your coffee/lunch, by listening to you and then giving you their advice, say 'thanks for your attention' or just 'thanks for being there'. What about your partner – how often do you thank them for sharing their life with you?

Inspirations for you:

'I can no other answer make, but, thanks, and thanks.'
William Shakespeare

'I feel a very unusual sensation – if it is not indigestion, I think it must be gratitude.'
Benjamin Disraeli

'Feeling gratitude and not expressing it is like wrapping a present and not giving it.'
William Arthur Ward

"If you
light a lamp
for somebody, it will also
brighten
your path."

Buddist saying

H *is for* How

can I
help *you*?

Insight for you

It's such a great question. 'How can I help you?'

Not, 'can I help you?' which – as a closed question (more on these in Q) – instinctively throws up a 'yes or no' in our minds. '*How* can I help you?' tells the other person to consider in what way you can help them; you know you can and you just want them to tell you *how*. '*What* can I do to help?' has the same effect – tell me *what* I can do to help, not *if* I can.

Here's the point. Helping other people first, putting yourself forward to lend a hand, to help, support and to give *first* is the key to helping people to help *you*. Less of the attitude of 'who can help me?' and 'what can they do to help me get this?' and more 'what can I do to help them?' Then ask them.

It's a nicer way to be in the world, to come from an angle of helping, supporting and collaborating with people. We can't get where we're going all by ourselves and nor do we want to anyway – despite what some people think. Even if we think we can, we can't. Somewhere along the line, every day we're relying on other people to help, support and collaborate with us. So let's go there *first*.

Interestingly, the more you help other people, support them, offer up help first, the more they naturally want to help you, and the key word in that is 'naturally'. Rather than feeling they *have* to help you. You may be 'the boss' or 'mum' or 'in charge' but if people don't *want* to help you, support you or collaborate with you naturally, then you're always going to have a harder time getting things done; being understood; being part of the team. Whichever team you're in, if people help and support you because they *want* to, it's so much quicker and easier.

There's a hugely important principle of influence that comes into play here. Reciprocity. 'The practice of exchanging things with others for mutual benefit'. The word *mutual* here is our key. It's not one-sided, it works both ways.

Two important points for you here.
Firstly, I recommend you read the brilliant book, which has 'influenced' me in so many ways – and still does. *Influence: The Science of Persuasion* by Dr Robert Cialdini. A book that encapsulates and clearly distinguishes the six principles of influence.

When I've discussed this book with clients (and encouraged them to go off and buy it) we've worked on the principles of influence together. Often they struggle at first with influence being 'manipulative'. Once we understand that we ourselves are influenced all day and every day by these same principles then, by understanding them, we can understand much more about how others are influenced too. Reciprocation is just one of the six principles Dr Cialdini defines.

The second point for you is that by offering to help someone *first*, by always looking for a way to 'go there first' – offering to make a coffee; picking up a sandwich for someone; helping someone find something out – it has a throw back to us. It makes *us* feel better.

It's a big part of being understood ourselves. Being remembered and recognised as someone who's helpful, supportive, collaborative is an easy way to be more promotable, to be the one who gets the business, to be given more opportunities because people, us included, like people like that. In business, the collaborative, supportive team-player will always – ultimately – go further than the lone-shark 'it's all about me' type. You know the ones I mean.

Now you may be thinking 'I'm a helpful person already, what's your point?' My point is to look for *more* ways to help people. Ask yourself 'How can I help that person?' – even just offering, helps you too. If we only give help when we're asked for it, when it's assumed we will; that's different. It's when we come from the position of offering it, regardless of whether it's needed, that things change for us. Trust me on this. I know it with every fibre in my body and I know it from the opportunities that come to my clients as they offer help first.

When I worked in a large London-based organisation, there was a lot of 'me, me, me – who can help *me* with this?' around. Interestingly, those of us who consistently tried to help other people, collaborated with others, did much better. I struggled sometimes with this principle, especially when time was short and tempers were frayed. You can only go so far by *telling* people to help you, by assuming they will. You go much further by offering to support and collaborate with others on their way *first*. Be the person who offers help, who comes forward, first.

Ideas for you to start working with today:

- Look for ways to offer help *first*. 'Let me help you with that', 'How can I help you with that?' 'Give that to me to finish.' You've got the idea. Go there first!

- Order yourself a copy of Dr Robert Cialdini's book. Seek him out on iTunes, and on YouTube.com. He makes the science of persuasion easy to understand and once understood, you will be so much more flexible in how you approach people and situations. You'll get the principle of Reciprocity nailed and it will open up all sorts of doors for you, I promise you. It has for me and still does, every day. It's become a natural default now. It will for you too if you want it to.

- Think about something you're struggling with or are stuck on. Think of who can help you, advise you, point you in the right direction and call or approach them. Tell them 'now I know you'll be able to help me with this.' For the most part, people love to be told they'll be able to help. Can you hear the subtle assumption that they definitely will be able to help. When you've explained – as clearly and succinctly as you can – you then say 'and you know I'll do the same for you.' You've put out the principle of reciprocation. Let's help each other on our ways, I've just happened to ask you first.

- How can I help *you*? Email me at **support@wayforwardsolutions.com** to let me know.

Inspirations for you:

'It is literally true that you can succeed best and quickest by helping others to succeed.'
Napolean Hill

'The more I help others succeed, the more I succeed.'
Ray Kroc

'The best place to find a helping hand is at the end of your arm.'
Swedish proverb

"Who cares? So what? What's in it for me?"

A Typical 10 Year Old

I *is for* I

Or do
I mean
you?

Insight for you

Now this is a 'belter' (*a loud, forceful song*). When you really get the sense of how powerful this principle is you'll be amazed at the difference it'll make for you.

> We've all been there, haven't we; either listening to or reading about someone telling you all the things *they* want, need, think, do.

Here we go – 'Well, I went here and I said that and then I did this and then I said that. Well, I mean, who do they think I am? I said 'well, I want to introduce this now' and I was adamant. So, I finally got what I wanted.' Now read that back and notice that, in reality, whilst a fairly strident bit of dialogue, it's entirely possible to hear that every day. The word 'I' appears eleven times – and not *once* does word 'we', 'you', 'us', 'our'.

Speaking like this is one thing. Dull. You can still pick up the 'I' clearly enough, but writing it like this is something else entirely. In written form, they're so easy to spot as we scan through a message – email, letter, report, article and too many instances of 'I, I, I' just switches people off. We all want to know where *we* fit in, how it affects *us*, what's in it for *us*.

Bart Simpson, the ever-cynical 10-year-old son in the TV show *'The Simpsons'* is a great example of 'Who cares? So what? What's in it for me?' Whilst it's a bit tough to see this, it *is* the filter most people use to sort through the myriad of information, opportunities and circumstances that come their way every day. If you know it and assume it to be true, then it helps you immediately to understand what people want from you, what they need to hear from you.

WII FM – What's In It For Me? It's been called something along the lines of 'the radio show everyone's listening to.'

So, be careful with the word I. 'I this, I that, I do' and *particularly* when it's in writing.

A client of mine showed me an email she'd sent out to her team. She couldn't understand why people were either ignoring it or the responses she got were very lukewarm.

Well, the message had nine paragraphs and *every* paragraph began with the word 'I'. So scanning it, it was easy to pick up the angle her nose was meeting the wind – it was all about her needs, wants and thoughts.

My client is a great learner, a great implementer and I'm so proud of her and all the big moves she makes moving herself and her team forward with a more savvy, influential communication style.

The moment we discussed this principle and she realised how she was coming across, she was firstly mortified and then adamant. 'That's the last time I send a message like that.' It was. She was promoted recently and one of the main reasons was because how company-centred she's considered to be and, for the money she now makes for the business. It's also noticed the extent to which her team support her and collaborate with her.

She thinks about 'we', 'they', 'our', 'us' all the time. Her 'I' is at the back now and she's more successful for it. She also comments that she likes *herself* better for it too!

Notice it. I this, I that, I think, I do, I want, I need and, let's be honest, here's the rub: People don't care so much about what *you* think, want and need as much as they care about what *they* think, want and need. Tough for some of us to hear I know, but, if we're really honest with ourselves, we know people really care about what *they* think, want and need. They are always – *as we are* – filtering it through 'WII FM?'

It's so powerful to know you don't need to be I, I, I all the time to have credibility and recognition.

By being more inclusive in your language, by including others in your thinking, requests, and your explanations there's another part of the secret. You include *them* in the responsibility too. You share the responsibility with others by implication. Which would you respond to more easily? 'I've got a tight deadline on this one, how can I get it sorted in time? What am I going to do?' *or* 'We've got a tight deadline on this one, how can we get this sorted in time? What ideas do you have?'

'My new client needs my input before the weekend. Who can I ask to help?' *or* 'Our new client need our input before the weekend. Who can we ask for help?' As one of my colleagues used to say 'it's a no-brainer, Kay.'

This is such an important piece for you to grab and use. Why would you want to exclude others in being involved, in the highs and lows, in the responsibility? Engage with us quickly and easily by including 'us' in your thinking.

So when *do* you use 'I'?

How *I* find it works is to make the story, issue etc., personal with 'I' and then relate it to 'we' so it becomes, for example 'I'm so thrilled I'm invited to X's meeting too. You know it's going to be good and we'll learn something about what's going on. I'll make sure the team knows the headlines as soon as I get back.' Notice how it's become less about 'I' and more about 'us' and 'them'.

'We', 'our', 'us' is inclusive language. It gives the listener/reader the sense that we're in this together, that they're included. 'We did', 'we know', 'as a company we're striving to', versus 'I', 'I'm', 'me', 'mine' and 'my' – for the listener/reader it becomes so, well, dull. Who wants to be thought of as dull or 'banging on about themselves?'

There's a great expression I want to pop in here for you, one that's stayed with me for years 'there's no I in team – but there's me, if you look hard enough.' A cute play on the words and a trick I know. You are in there, you are part of the team – whatever your team happens to be, professional, family, sports, friends but it's not all about you, is it?

My niece, Grace, aged 14 as I write this, told me that our regular chats are to be 'all about us, you and me – but mostly about me.' She's 14 so it goes with the territory but for us older and wiser ones, it's all about you, isn't it – or in our case, it's all about *them*. Now.

Ideas for you to start working with today:

- Each time you start to speak or write and feel 'I' coming up, ask yourself if it could be made into 'we' or 'our' or 'you' and 'your'.

- After you've typed out an email, report, quick note, just check that you've put across how your message affects the other person and not just you; what you consider they might want or need. Something like 'understanding that this may mean XYZ to you, it may help to etc' or '*you*'ll notice that this is on a Friday so *we*'ve got plenty of time to prepare *our*selves etc.' Can you see, you've told the reader you're thinking about them, you're including them – and yourself – and *they*'re on *your* mind. They're also *sharing* in the responsibility. Aha.

- Watch how you start your paragraphs i.e. how many times 'I' appears first – certainly in your emails. Emailing helpfully using short clearly set out paragraphs, bullets etc – it's easy to scan and see all the times the word 'I' appears. Again with practice, switching them, noticing where it could be '*we*' or '*us*' or '*you*'. You'll become a much more influential communicator just with that subtle but powerful tweak. It's *huge* in fact.

- If 'I' immediately springs up for you; notice how – as you practice – you can switch the focus and change it to 'you' or 'your' and notice the difference – you're sending out a completely different message to the other person. What's in it for them?

Inspirations for you:

The 6 most important words:
    'I admit I made a mistake.'

The 5 most important words:
    'You did a good job.'

The 4 most important words:
    'What is your opinion?'

The 3 most important words:
    'If you please.'

The 2 most important words:
    'Thank You.'

The 1 most important word:
    'We.'

The least important word:
    'I.'

Unknown

'The ratio of *I* to *We* is the best indicator as to the level of a team.'
Louis B. Ergen

'He must increase, but I must decrease.'
John 3:30

> "What **soap** is to the **body**, **laughter** is to the **soul**."

Yiddish proverb

J *is for* Joker

Humour is *such* a secret sauce

Insight for you

'You don't stop laughing because you grow old, you grow old because you stopped laughing.'

Michael Pritchard

Who wants to grow 'old' or be thought of as 'growing old' – we're all *getting* older but the key here is in the language. Getting older is happening to all of us, the newborn baby born yesterday is older today. To *grow old* brings up completely different feelings and images than *older*.

We're born being naturally open to laughter. You can hear children laughing and openly bursting out laughing in any playground, cinema, restaurant and they're naturally programmed to find things funny. Think how easy it is to make a child giggle just by tickling them or even making out that you're going to tickle them; they start laughing *in anticipation* of being tickled.

As we 'grow up' (now there's a leading statement for a start) we often lose the natural gift of laughter and of finding things funny every day. We think we have to be more serious and we do, but not all the time and definitely not at the risk of being old before our time. People can literally forget to laugh or forget *how* to laugh. It's *not* funny.

Being 6ft tall as I am, I definitely *grew up* but remembering to be playful, to find and even look for the funny side of things is definitely one of my secret sauces when working with people, when negotiating and just generally chatting with people. My dad had an easy way about him and was able to make people laugh both *at* him and *with* him – that's part of the secret. Be prepared to laugh at yourself, not just at others. Start with finding yourself funny. You are funny, things you do, say, think, assume. They're funny and I mean you can make them funny, share them. Go there first – people *love* to laugh with you and sharing something about yourself where you've tripped up or got yourself into a muddle, it helps people to relax.

Finding things funny *and* encouraging others to do so too, is a big part of being remembered and recognised as someone people want to have around.

I don't mean that you turn into the court jester, the clown, but rather that you allow yourself to both laugh and 'crack up' whenever you can. At work this is a big part of getting along with others. Laughing *with* people (not at, *with*) is an easy path to establishing rapport. It breaks the ice and gets you on side with someone if you both find something funny. Look for opportunities to laugh.

Laughing relaxes us; it can diffuse tricky situations to be able to laugh – even if it's just a smile.

One of my friends was in a Stand-Up Comedians competition and told me how he found that the best description of where comedy and laughter starts is to imagine you have a train going along a track, it's doing what it should be doing, moving along nicely and everything's just normal. Suddenly, it veers off the track. That's where the laughter is, when the story veers off the track.

Think about telling a story along the lines of 'I was coming here this morning and we're all sitting there on the bus. As normal, no one's speaking and we're all either listening to our podcasts or reading the paper or sleeping. Suddenly, a chap gets up and starts singing to the girl next to him about how he's noticed her every day and wants to take her out for a meal and none of us knew where to look' and the story continues. The train coming off the track was the moment we thought about someone standing up and starting to sing on the bus. We could imagine it and it's immediately out-of-the ordinary; embarrassing (great recipe for laughter) and we're involved.

My point of putting J for Joker here on our journey from A to Z is to remind you that it's good to laugh and to look for ways of making other people laugh. It makes connecting with people quicker and easier for you.

You can diffuse a situation, make another person feel relaxed, make yourself feel relaxed by just picking up on a comment and allowing it to either make you laugh or laughing about it with other people.

One of the first things you'll notice about a good speaker is that they'll very quickly try to establish rapport with the audience by making them laugh. Often making the audience laugh about a situation they have in common or making them laugh about themselves. It's a subtle way to start to have the audience 'on side'.

Remember too about releasing serotonin – we can produce more serotonin from one minute of laughter than we can from ten minutes exercising. So laughter really is the best medicine.

Ideas for you to start working with today:

- When you think something sounds funny, laugh. Look for opportunities to laugh today, then tomorrow, then the next day. Instead of just smiling or smirking (yes, we've all done it) laugh instead.

- Notice other people and how often – and indeed *if* – they laugh and notice what they laugh at. You know I don't mean nervous giggling, I mean laughing using your tummy, your shoulders, your funny bones.

- Hire a DVD or find a few clips on YouTube which always make you smile. Maybe look up comedians from comedy shows that you've always found funny and remind yourself how good it is to laugh.

- When you're in a meeting or sitting with colleagues and you hear or think something's amusing, depending on the circumstances (clearly some are more appropriate than others) comment or if someone makes a joke, again – context – give yourself permission to laugh. Let's laugh more and lighten up some of our conversations this way (and often light up someone else's day at the same time).

Inspirations for you:

'To truly laugh, you must be able to take your pain, and play with it!'
Charlie Chaplin

'Laughter gives us distance. It allows us to step back from an event, deal with it and then move on.'
Bob Newhart

'When people are laughing, they're generally not killing each other.'
Alan Alda

Piglet sidled up to
Pooh from behind.

'Pooh!' he whispered.

'Yes, Piglet?'

'Nothing,' said Piglet,
taking Pooh's paw.
'I just wanted to be
sure of you.'

A.A. Milne
Winnie the Pooh

is for Keep-in-touch

The fortune's in the follow up

Insight for you

It's so easy, isn't it? 'Well, I called and left her a message' or 'Yes, I sent an email last week about it.' 'They said they'd do it by Friday, I wonder what's happening?' They're all phrases we can all hear ourselves saying.

Well, you may _ask_ people to do things for you, you may even _tell_ them to do them, they may have said 'OK' to you but keeping in touch, checking in, following up – these are the ways for you to actually _know_ what's going on.

The other part of 'keep in touch' is literally just that. As well as following up on things, keeping in touch, being the person who makes the first move (and doesn't wait and think, 'oh, it's their turn to call me') is another huge part of being noticed, of being thought of, and getting things done. The word 'touch' is just right for what I want to share with you here. 'Touch' is 'the act of bringing a part of one's body into contact with someone or something' and 'an act of lightly pressing or striking something in order to move or operate it.'

Both of those definitions are relevant for us here. To bring you into contact with someone and to lightly press someone in order to move him or her. You know what I'm saying here – to keep in touch is to stay in the other person's consciousness, you're on their radar, you're interested and involved in what's going on. You haven't just pressed 'send' or said 'call me when it's done please' and left it to them. You're telling the other person that you're interested and invested in what happens next.

So often clients say to me 'well they never tell me what's going on.' Have you asked them? 'well they've said they'd do it.' Do you *always* do what you say you'll do, when you say you'll do it? Hmm, I don't.

I'm not suggesting you turn into a *Woodpecker* and call people or email people every half an hour asking 'what's happening?' 'when will it be ready?' 'have you done it yet?' No. What I *am* suggesting is far more subtle and effective.

A big learning here for us is the power of managing other people's expectations. You're in a meeting. You're asked 'how is XYZ project going? 'Er, I'm not sure, John's working on it. I think it's going OK.' Can you hear how wishy-washy and unsure you sound?

You're at your desk and a call comes to meet a client who's popped in and wants to discuss their account. You've no idea what's happening with their account as your colleague is working on it and they're in a meeting at the moment. You can get the idea. Keeping in the loop, keeping in touch, keeping involved. You *manage expectations* and that's all part of being someone who can be trusted and relied upon, some-one who knows, as the expression goes 'their arse from their elbow.'

By managing expectations, by keeping in touch and having an up-to-date position on what's happening, you'll always be ahead of the person who has to shrug their shoulders and say 'I don't know, I'll go and find out.'

A great example of how keeping in touch and managing expecta-tions makes a difference, is our Underground system here in London. When I first used to commute to work in London, we'd arrive on the platform and stand and stare at a black hole, the tunnel, until the train came. The only way to understand how long since the last train had left i.e. there *should* be another one along soon – was by judging how many people were on the platform. It seems so antiquated now and, of course, it was.

We used to have no idea how long we'd have to wait or, indeed, *if* a train was coming at all. We just had to hope and assume. Now we have the monitors on each platform with 'ticker tape' running across them. With 'Next train in 2 minutes' we have our expectations managed and London Underground is keeping in touch with us. We can decide whether to wait, whether to buy a paper or whether just to walk. Working with clients I often use this comparison when discussing how – *and if* – they keep in touch with their colleagues and clients. Do you want your colleagues or your boss to be staring into a black hole? How do your clients feel, what do they think about you when you leave them hanging around on the platform?

So, going forward, a quick call '*knowing* you said you'd have this ready by Friday, just wondering how you're getting on.' Can you feel how subtle a touch this is and yet how powerful too? What we're actually saying here is 'you said you'd have it ready by Friday, will it be?' but the *way* it's said is lighter, more of a touch. We're saying we both know you made a commitment to Friday and the 'wondering' is so much less confrontational than 'and I want to know, have you done it yet?'

The secret sauce of thinking like this now is also that you buy yourself a huge piece of credit if things are slightly or even very 'off track'. Having kept in touch, along the way, you're able to follow that 'no surprises' edict.

Someone I worked for in my own corporate background had a mantra about managing our clients' expectations 'tell them what's happening Kay, even if nothing's happening, *tell them* nothing's happening.' Make sure your clients aren't staring into their screens (*the black hole*) hoping or wondering 'what's happening?'

An email, 'how's the project XYZ going? Let me know if I can add anything or you need anything from me.' Even if you know the person has all they need, your 'touch' acts as a prompt and a reminder *without* you being the dreaded *Woodpecker*. (By the way, I love Woodpeckers. They're hard-working, shy, effective and the sound of them is a sure sign of spring.) The action of a Woodpecker, the constant drilling, is what we want to avoid as we keep in touch and follow up with people.

We want a *lighter* touch. From your toolbox, this will be less your drill or hammer and more your feather duster.

In our friendships, calling the person you're thinking about just to say 'I was thinking of you and thought I'd give you a call' is such a light, friendly and lovely thing to say. We all love to be thought of, to be remembered by others. It makes us feel good too, to tell someone else we're thinking of him or her.

When you've met someone either at an event, on a plane, a networking meeting, rather than pop their card in a drawer, drop them an email or give them a call. They have a choice, of course, as to whether they want to keep in touch, we all do. The point here though is to *go there first*. Make the first move. 'The fortunes are in the follow up.' So stay on the radar, stay connected, stay in touch and go there first by making the first move and following up.

Ideas for you to start working with today:

- Think of someone who you're waiting to hear from or whose 'turn' you think it is to get in touch. Get in touch with them first. Say 'I was thinking about you this morning and wondering how you are' or 'how you're getting on with XYZ?' – well, you are thinking about them so it's all true and you're making the first move now. No more waiting around for you anymore.

- If there's something you're either stuck with or your waiting to hear from someone on something you're working on – think back as to when you heard from them last, what the next step agreed was and then 'touch' them with either a call or an email. 'What's happening with XYZ, I want to make sure *we're* on track with it.'

- Make it part of your daily routine to use your feather duster to 'touch' people so you keep up-to-date, so you're on their mind and not somewhere down their list. Send them a link, for example, to something you know they're interested in – it's a little prompt, a reminder about you, you pop up on their radar. They'll soon get used to you being this way and rather than wait for you to ask, they'll start to tell you where they are and what's going on with things. You've told them – without telling them – you want to know, you're staying involved, you're on the case, you're around, you're thinking about them. They'll want to manage your expectations.

- Understanding what's going on, how people are getting on, is a huge piece of being understood. The next time you hear yourself in your head say 'hmm, I wonder when that's going to be ready?' or 'I wish they'd let me know what's happening with XYZ' – make it your business to find out. It is your business to find out anyway, you're involved, so stay that way. Waiting around and hoping to hear, hoping for the best isn't the way forward anymore, is it?

Inspirations for you:

'Success comes from taking the initiative and following up – persisting – eloquently expressing the depth of your love. What simple action could you take today to produce a new momentum towards success in your life?'
Anthony Robbins

'What tribes are, is a very simple concept that goes back 50 million years. It's about leading and connecting people and ideas. And it's something that people have wanted forever.'
Seth Godin

'The only exercise some people get is jumping to conclusions, running down their friends, side-stepping responsibility, and pushing their luck!'
Author Unknown

"When people talk, listen completely. Most people never listen.

Ernest Hemingway

is for Listen

Shhh!

Insight for you

'We have two ears and one mouth so that we can listen twice as much as we speak.'

Epictetus, Greek philosopher c. AD 55–c.135

This quote had to go first. Listen twice as much as we speak and we've got this principle nailed. Look at the time when it was written and it's *still* just as relevant today as it was then. I put it here first for you so we're squarely on the same page with the message, straight off.

We've all got something to say; we all want to be heard, to get our message across to those around us. We all want to contribute – don't we? We all want to add to things. We all want to be understood. What we all want to avoid though is to 'bang on' (a great expression my husband Snowy uses). To be that person who dominates a conversation or sucks up the time in a meeting so there's little time for anyone else.

Two points here to bring out.

Firstly, to listen doesn't mean just waiting for your turn to speak. It means to give your attention to someone or something. Give your attention – not wait for the pause.

This is so important to define, laying it out here for you is to remind you of all the times you've told a story or put a point across and the *second* you've finished (and often *before*) someone grabs the pause and says something like 'yes, that reminds me of when I etc' or 'I've got something to say on that etc' or, worse still, 'I can top that' as if it's a competition.

They've been *waiting* to speak and not really listening to you. We've all experienced it and it gets on our nerves and actually can really rile us, and close us down. We can often see the person nodding and starting to open their mouth to 'tell' us what they think *before* we've even finished.

Listening more and speaking less is so much better. *Giving* our attention to the other person will help make us someone others want to be around. Being understood by other people as a person who gives their full attention.

Secondly – and here's a *big* piece about being understood. We *learn* so much more.

- We *learn* about what's going on with the other person and/or the situation.

- We *learn* about how the other person is thinking; what their position is on something *before* we commit ourselves to our own position.

- We *pick up* on things that are going on whilst the other person is speaking that often define what – if anything – we want to say about the subject.

- We give ourselves time to think – something that is so often undervalued. Time to think and decide *if* we actually want to respond or if we want to ask a few more questions. Let's show we're interested, because we are – aren't we? We're interested in the other person.

Understanding others, understanding a situation better, understanding what's going on or what went on is all about being able to be better understood ourselves. The way we do that, is to listen more than we speak and *ask* more than we *tell*.

The 'Q' in this book is all about Questions and using good questions is a game changer. We'll explore that in 'Q' but I just wanted you to know you'll have the questions up your sleeve, which will help you be an even better listener.

We're all work-in-progress. I know I am – and anyway, who wants to be the finished article? Listening more than speaking is something I work on too. Especially when we're passionate about our subject.

Because so many people speak more than they listen, when you actually give someone your attention, show them you're interested by wanting to hear more from them, by inviting them to tell you more, often they're quite shocked.

A great analogy for you is from my dear father. Dad was a good storyteller and he was also a good listener. He was very popular with a great ear for an accent he could impersonate and he had a fun sense of humour.

We often used to have to tell Dad to stop so we could breathe when we ate together as a family. His stories came from listening to other people's stories and then repeating them with his own spin.

Dad used to be in the Royal Air Force and was part of the crew flying Lancaster planes. He would often use plane-related expressions in everyday life. He'd say 'we're clear for takeoff' if we were all ready to go out or 'chocks away' etc when we were off. Dad knew the trick of being a good listener was to be more 'a receiver' than 'a transmitter'.

If you think of two-way radio you transmit the message and then click another button and start to receive the answer back. Hit 'receive' *more* than you hit 'transmit' then, that's the message. Have your 'receive' button on and then decide, as and when – and if – to hit 'transmit'.

This reminds me of one of those moments, which I'm sure you'll have had too. At a cocktail party, I was stuck – and I mean *stuck* – with a chap who was literally transmitting to me about how great he was, how much he'd done in his life, how much he'd earned, the car he drove etc. You get the idea. I was getting to the stage of needing to send up rescue flares to anyone who was around. I'd asked him a few questions at first, genuinely interested in him. Then, I felt my interest wane and my hackles rise.

In the twenty or so minutes he had 'banged on' at me he didn't ask me *one* question about what I do, where I live, how I knew the hosts, nothing. He paused for a second to have a sip of his drink – his throat was probably dry after talking *at* me for all that time – and so I asked him 'So David (let's call him David for the purpose of our story) what would you like to ask me?' David did have the good grace to cough and look a bit uncomfortable for a split second to gather himself. 'Oh, yes, er what did you say you do?' 'I didn't David because you didn't ask me and now I'm going to go and circulate, I know you'll understand.'

This is 100% true and I'd do it again. It proved my point about what happens to the person on the receiving end – me in this case – I closed down, felt fed up and couldn't wait to move on. As the phrase goes, when someone like that says to you 'Oh see you again soon' you think to yourself 'not if I see you first!' Well if you think you might be someone like David, you're always going to make it harder for yourself because other people want to avoid people like that.

Listening to others and sharing the transmit/receive button is a big part of being someone others want to be around; being remembered as someone who is as interested as they are interesting themselves. We know when we're transmitting too much; we can read the signs. Often the other person has 'Help' written across their face.

Two ears, one mouth for a reason. Remember.

Ideas for you to start working with today:

- Make a deal with yourself – 'today, when I can, I'll listen more than I'll speak.' An easy way to make sure you're listening and not looking for your opportunity to respond is to repeat, in your head, what the person is saying as they're saying it. When I first started working with clients it was a great way for me to stay with them and drown out the worried voice saying 'oh, what will I say?' It works. It slows you down in a good way and helps you absorb what's being said to you. Helps you to remember the details.

- So, you've heard and listened to someone's story or opinion on something and when the person pauses or looks for a response, you nod and ask them a question about what they've just said – 'that's interesting, what happened then?' or 'wow, how do you think that happened?' or 'tell me a bit more about that'.

- This is, of course, dependent on time and context – standing in the middle of a busy road waiting for the lights to go green is probably not the time to say 'tell me a bit more.' It's about being open to hearing and listening to the other person and, trust me, freeing yourself from the need to always have a response, another story, an 'I can top that' angle.

- When you *ask* as opposed to *tell*, it helps you weed out the people who are really interested in you. Notice as you ask people a bit more or don't automatically go back with your story, notice *if* they ask you anything. You'll soon find out the people who are interested in you as opposed to those who want to use you as a mirror in which to reflect themselves. They're the dull ones. They haven't thought long enough about what it is to be interested, really interested, in another person.

Inspirations for you:

'Listening well is as powerful a means of communication and influence as to talk well.'

John Marshall

'A wise old owl sat on an oak; The more he saw the less he spoke; The less he spoke the more he heard; Why aren't we like that wise old bird?'

Unknown

'Courage is what it takes to stand up and speak; courage is also what it takes to sit down and listen.'

Winston Churchill

Meanings are
not determined
by situations,
but we determine ourselves by
the meanings
we give to situations.

Alfred Adler

M *is for* Meaning

We're
meaning-
seeking
machines

Insight for you

Well, what I *mean* by that is we naturally go inside our heads when we hear, read, see something and try to put meaning around it.

Put context or a framework around
something to make it make sense.

This is a really important part of our journey together. Knowing that we are all always seeking, naturally, the meaning for us, for others, for a situation in what is happening around us.

Putting it here for you under M is to make sure that from this point, you're aware (you notice what you notice) about your own search for meaning. So, because you now know you're a meaning-seeking machine, you can help others understand both you, and themselves, more by *giving* them your meaning. Sometimes it's actively useful to let others make up their own minds as to 'what it means' but more often than not, especially in the workplace, it's more helpful and time-saving to give people that framework.

'In other words...', 'by that I mean...' 'so this will mean...' 'or we could say...'. Can you hear that by using those phrases, which are very normal and easy on the ear, you naturally offer your listener or reader a bit more information? Give them more of an opportunity to 'get it'.

Too often people take things as face value and nod thinking 'Heyho, I'll have to find out later what that means' or 'I've no idea what he or she just said but hopefully it won't matter.' Well it does. It matters a lot when we want to make sure we're understood, that people take on our ideas, our opinions and do so easily. It's simple too.

Everyday, we're translating what someone has said or written or done and making our own sense of it. Notice the *'our own'* sense of it. *Your* sense of something will be different to mine because we're different. What we can do to bridge that difference is to ensure, as far as we can, that we offer enough information – often said one way and then another way – to make it easy for the other person to understand us. *By that I mean* clarify or expand a bit.

A prime example of this is when Snowy, my long-suffering husband and life-long case study, says to me something like 'Oh, XYZ happened today' and just stops. Immediately, I hear in my head 'and?' or 'because?' and we're married. He now knows to give me one more sentence with some context about 'why' that happened or 'what it means'.

What about your colleagues; your team; you boss; your clients wherever they are in the world and however you contact them? They will have the same sort of questions popping up in their heads too. They do and will. So answer the questions naturally up front. *In other words* give them the meaning – the consequences or the background.

Just a bit, not a whole essay, just a bit. The headlines. If they want more they'll ask you – especially if you ask them 'I hope that's clear?' or 'does that make sense?' What you've done is remove those questions left hanging there.

So what does this *mean* for you? Well it means you'll get clearer too about what *you* think something means. For the other person it may mean something else but they'll understand you more, your point of view, your position. As they respond 'and it could also mean' or 'actually, I think XYZ' you'll find yourselves naturally discussing something that might have just been stated and left hanging without either of you really understanding what you meant to say.

You'll hear these phrases 'well, what I meant to say was' or 'I'm sorry, what I really mean is' and 'he or she just didn't get what I meant'. You can avoid both having to say these phrases and having them said about you. You can also avoid wasting all the time and energy it takes to clear up the confusion that can be caused. Now that *means* something, doesn't it?

Ideas for you to start working with today:

- Be ready to use 'by that I mean' and 'in other words' or 'i.e.' and those sort of expressions which immediately tell the other person you're going to make sure they know what you mean – without patronizing them.

- Notice when someone else makes a statement without the context, the meaning – notice firstly if anyone else asks and notice *if* you automatically ask yourself 'I wonder what he or she means by that?' If you think it's appropriate and there's time, ask. 'Can you just tell me a bit more about that please' or 'what will that mean, please?' You'll tell both the person and anyone else involved that you don't just take things at face value, you're prepared to dig a bit deeper, you want to understand and you do it in a natural, inquisitive way.

- You'll have noticed the '*please*' – that's crucial. To avoid your question being confrontational and to be more about informa-tion-gathering, the 'please' is not only polite but it's *essential*. It makes it a request and not a demand. We all respond much more easily to requests and less so to demands. By that I mean, requests are desires, and demands are instructions. Which do you prefer to receive?

Inspirations for you:

'The least of things with a meaning is worth more in life than the greatest of things without it.'
Carl Gustav Jung

'Meaning is not what you start with, but what you end up with.'
Peter Elbow

'If you can't explain it simply, you don't know it well enough.'
Albert Einstein

Yes and **No** are
very short
        words to say,
but we should think for
some length of time
before saying them.

Unknown

N *is for* No

Or do
you mean
Yes?

Insight for you

'No, no, no I don't want to do that, thank you' or 'No, that's not it' or 'No, I can't do that now'. Hearing the word 'no' before hearing anything else is both a day-to-day occurrence and it's something we can avoid – or certainly choose – whether we say it *first*. Or not.

The second we hear 'no' we hear resistance and we know, intuitively, we have either a battle on our hands or we have encountered defiance, opposition or disagreement with what we've said, suggested or with what we believe. No. You only have to read it like that – on its own like that – to get how powerful it is to hear it, especially when you hear it first, before anything else.

We may well disagree, we may hear ourselves say inside 'No, that's wrong, this is right' or 'No, there's no way I'm doing that' but what we do when we put it out there *first*, is we immediately put the other person either in the position of being wrong, daft or rejected. They are strong words – wrong, daft or rejected. It's fair to say that all of us want to avoid feeling we are in the wrong, feeling that the other person thinks we're daft or, worse still, feeling rejected.

Here's a great example that happened to me recently when chatting with a friend who was juggling timing to get to Heathrow Airport. I said 'If you want to you can stay at our house, park your car here and grab a cab to the airport from here.' He immediately said 'No, no, no. It's much better to leave my car at the airport. It's just a pain to drive there etc.'

Can you hear in that offer I made, how the first thing that came back to me was 'no'? 'No' that won't work, no I'm not interested, 'no' you don't understand. I felt as if I'd been *brushed off* and my offer rejected, almost like it was a daft and silly suggestion, a waste of time.

What it was, in fact, was an offer to help someone out and here's a suggestion how it could work.

He could have so easily said 'Yes, thanks Kay, that's an idea. It's actually easier to drive straight to the airport. A long drive but easier in the long run.' What a difference. Let's consider what this way of responding does.

'Yes' tells me 'I hear you and acknowledge what you've said.' 'Thanks' tells me 'you made an offer and I appreciate it.' Those two signs are out there with me, first. There with me before I hear what your decision is. Yes and thanks. Easy. Now I really like this chap and I knew he didn't mean to make me feel silly or rebuffed *and* yet he did. That was just a suggestion with no attachment to it i.e. if he wanted to stay, fine, if not, that was fine too.

Calling this part of the book – No (or do I mean Yes?) – is to remind us that we can say, 'Yes' even if ultimately we mean 'No'. We can say 'yes' first. And, we can *say* 'Yes' in a number of ways too. So what I'm saying here in essence too is we can say 'no' without saying it and we can say 'yes' without saying it too. It's useful.

Yes/No are positions of right/wrong or will/won't or good/bad or black/white. They are both ends of a spectrum and we don't have to answer with yes/no – even if we've been asked a question which naturally prompts us to say it, particularly 'No'. We can say 'Yes' first and then lead on to 'actually, no'.

Why? Because it's a smoother, kinder, easier way for the other person to take on what is, in effect, rejection. Rejection of an idea; a suggestion; a thought; an offer. We all inherently want to avoid rejection. We all want to be included, acknowledged, understood. So to know that about ourselves is to understand the same about everyone else too. We acknowledge the other person's offer, their opinion, their contribution by saying 'yes' first.

'No' is a small, quick word *loaded* with the potential to upset, close down, rebuff a person when – most of the time – it's the last thing we want or mean to do. 'Do you want to come to dinner on Friday with us?' 'No thanks, we're out that night, what a shame.' You've answered a direct, closed question i.e. one that has a yes or no answer and you've said 'no' you're already booked. Also, this is a pretty easy situation, one that doesn't have much emotion or consequence attached to it. OK – *and* – it still could have been said like this: 'Thanks for asking, what a lovely idea. We're out on Friday so we'll have to miss it.' With this example, you haven't even had to say 'No'. You said 'Thanks' first – which is 'Yes' in disguise (yes, I acknowledge your offer, yes I hear you, yes that sounds nice). Saying it's a nice idea – told the other person it's a kind offer. *Then*, told them you're already booked.

In the workplace, in negotiation situations (at home, just as at work) can you get the sense of how powerful this is for you? 'Yes, that's an idea. I'm already booked that night but thanks for asking me.' (It could have been 'No, I'm out that night.')

'Yes, I hear what you say. Let me think about it. When do you need an answer by?' (It could have been 'No, that doesn't sound like it'll work. Let me think about it etc.') 'Yes, we could go to the client and say that. We could also wait until tomorrow.' (It could have been 'No, we can't say that. Let's wait until tomorrow.')

It takes – like all these principles – a moment of thought *before* responding and it takes practice but it makes such a difference when you acknowledge the person's idea/position *first* with 'yes' before going on to comment and to respond with your own answer, suggestion or comment.

I want to put to you that it's an easier way to get along with people, to keep people on your side and it's all about being understood at that visceral – gut, intuitive, primal – level if you accept the other person and what they're saying or suggesting *before* you come back with your own response, be it yes or no.

Ideas for you to work with today:

- Notice how many times your instinct is to say 'no' first when someone says something, emails you something, when you read something.

- Now notice how many times people say it to you. 'No but' and 'No that's not it' 'no, I can't do that' and start to notice the effect it has on you. Imagine them saying 'yes' to you instead of the 'no'. Yes acknowledges what you've said, and your position – it doesn't have to mean 'yes I agree'.

- Watch out for head-shaking 'no' before saying anything. Just as powerful, the other person *knows* (and so do you if someone's doing it to you) that you're about to say 'no' and they haven't even finished speaking. It's really off-putting and you're already saying 'no' before you've given them time to explain.

- 'Yes, I can understand how you might think that' or 'Yes, that's an interesting idea' or 'Yes, that sounds tricky.' Easy phrases which start your response off *without* you saying 'No' first. Say them out aloud first so you can hear and feel yourself say the words. Make it your deal with this principle that you'll say 'yes' to people as much as you can before you come back with your response, objection or idea. Yes?

- 'Yes, you can do this' and 'Yes, it will make a difference for you' and 'Yes, I'm work in progress too.'

Inspirations for you:

'The warrior's approach is to say "yes" to life: "Yea" to it all.'
Joseph Campbell

'The highest form of ignorance is when you reject something you don't know anything about.'
Wayne Dyer

'Never allow a person to tell you no who doesn't have the power to say yes.'
Eleanor Roosevelt

Tell me and
I'll forget;
show me and
I may remember;
involve me and
I'll understand.

Chinese Proverb

O *is for* Openness

Or are you a 'need to know' type?

Insight for you

There's an expression we hear a lot at the moment 'TMI' – 'is that TMI?' or 'oh my goodness, it was just TMI' – too much information. Used when someone tells you something which has either too much detail or they touch on something just too personal (for example, the step-by-step detail of their recent Doctor's appointment) or their intimate relationship details.

Putting O for Openness here is about putting it to you to be prepared to share information and details *without* straying into TMI territory. It's really about:

> Giving people more of yourself to be able to connect with you.

So giving people more of what they need from you to take action and feel comfortable.

This is where some of my clients' 'Jedi' references come in because when you're able to connect with people quickly and easily, mystical things happen for you that seem to give you *supernormal* powers.

When you can connect *with* people, you're able to get things done, find things out, work alongside people with their hearts as well as their minds; they *want* to work with you as opposed to just *having* to. It's not about just being the boss; it's about collaborating, sharing. You get noticed for getting things done easily.

It's about sharing some of your story, your interests, your disasters or trip ups (and yes, they're compelling and connecting; as much as, if not more so than your achievements because they make you *real*).

If I was to tell you that writing this book had been super-easy, the words just flew out of me and it was all done in less than a month you'd probably say 'OK, good for you' or 'I don't believe you Kay but OK, that's your story.' If I told you that 'it was a scary, exciting and an often daunting project; that sometimes I wanted to throw myself on the floor sobbing but once I really got started it spurred me on at the same time. It's made me feel exposed and uncomfortable at times but I carried on anyway and here it is.' Well, you're more likely to think 'yes, I can imagine that' or 'yes, and good for you, you've still done it, despite feeling like that.' It makes me more real. It's true by the way, the second part.

I've learned, by watching people who connect and engage with others really quickly and easily, what they're doing that really works. I've also learned by working with, and for, people who definitely make things difficult for themselves as they flail about, unable to get people on side with them or to see their point of view and watch them get more and more frustrated and confused. I've also learned by being able to distinguish these things in myself, noticing more what I'm doing that works and becoming clear so that now, I can show other people how to do the same.

Being more open to others about what's actually happening; why it's happening and some of the struggles along the way. It makes you real; it connects you. The more connected you are with people around you, the people you email, the people you call and the people you touch, however you do that, every day – the better your results will be. And, the more connected and *real* you'll feel.

There's a subtle blend here, a bit of a cocktail in fact – of mixing your credibility (what you've achieved, what you're involved in, what's good) together with your vulnerability (the struggles, the slip-ups, the concerns you have).

No one wants to hear someone 'bang on' about how great they are for very long. We also want to hear the struggles, the learning, the 'I need help with this' parts too. The same applies to leaving out the credibility and just banging on about how tough everything is. Dull and depressing. Being more open is mixing in the two. Just like a cocktail – too much or not enough of one of the components makes it undrinkable.

Here's an example of how *not* to connect with people around you. A few years ago, I worked with a client who was a newly-promoted senior manager and she was struggling to get her team to act on her requests; to respond and keep her updated and she said at the time she felt like 'an alien' to the team. Powerful language and just reading this you can guess it was a pretty uncomfortable position for her to be in.

Saying something to me along the lines of 'I only tell them what they need to know so it doesn't confuse them and they really don't need to know much.' Talk about alarm bells going off. She explained to me that during one of her recent team meetings she'd introduced a new public campaign being launched and commented that the meeting seemed to 'close down' when she said something along the lines of 'we haven't decided how you're going to take this forward. We're discussing it at the moment. When we do we'll get back to you.'

No request for input, no collaboration, no 'what do you think and here's what I think.' She separated herself by aligning herself with the management with 'we'll' and positioned the team as 'you'. Disconnected. Amazing, and yet, sadly not so amazing. This particular client never really got how she was making this situation for herself. She could only put the blame outside of herself. We didn't work together for very long. Heyho. As the saying goes 'you can take a horse to water but you can't make it drink.'

This type of point-and-tell, drip-feed style of operating is still so common. It's just so outdated and ineffective. You only have to ask a person who adopts this style how *they* like to be managed, how *they* like to be kept in the loop – we all want the same. Updates; honesty; information; contribution; a voice.

Consistently, the companies people want to work for as well as the people that we want to work for, and with, *include* us. They want our input, want to keep us posted about what's going on, the direction we're heading in. What these companies and their people don't do is adopt the so-called 'Mushroom Management' style – *feed them manure and keep them in the dark.*

You know by now; I don't mean you have to tell people every-single-thing that's going on; the highs/the lows; your excitement/your fears. Of course I don't. What I do mean is to share 'the headlines' more openly and expect to, be prepared to. What's happening both with yourself and the projects you and people around you are working on. Keep people up-dated, keep them in the loop.

Remember in 'K for Keep in Touch' – just a *touch* from you is often enough, a quick update, a 'we're still waiting to hear about XYZ' i.e. you're telling someone what's happening even if nothing's actually happening. You've told them, you've been open and for that you'll get credit from them for *being* open about it. I promise, it's a big part of you being understood.

Ideas for you to work with today:

- Notice today how much information people give you and what level is 'enough'. Some will say 'yes' or 'no' to a question and it may be enough for you. You'll also notice when you still have a question in your mind and – if it feels right and there's the opportunity – ask it. Trust yourself and ask for more. (See Q for Questioning, great questions and the *how to* and the *when* too). Know that filling in your 'gaps' will help you act on the information and be more effective. Remember, the quality of the questions often depends on the effectiveness of the answer. You'll often be asked a crappy question (I'll define them for you in Q) – but you get to *choose* if you give a crappy answer.

- When you're offering information yourself today, when someone asks you something – take a second to think about what they really *need* from you. Of course, sometimes it is just a 'yes' or 'no'. Mostly they need a couple more sentences from you; some context (P for Point will help you nail how to do this effectively) – framework or background to the situation – and then your thoughts or position; then the 'what next'.

- The point of this chapter, of O for Openness, is to avoid withholding information that people actually need to feel comfortable; to trust you; to move forward. Notice when you're withholding. We know when we are and so do other people. Ask yourself what's behind it and how it's affecting the other person.

Inspirations for you:

'If people are informed they will do the right thing. It's when they are not informed that they become hostages to prejudice.'
Charlayne Hunter-Gault

'New opinions often appear first as jokes and fancies, then as blasphemies and treason, then as questions open to discussion and finally as established truths.'
George Bernard Shaw

'Be who you are and say what you feel, because those who mind don't matter, and those who matter don't mind.'
Dr Seuss

"To talk much
and arrive nowhere
is the same as
climbing a tree
to catch a fish."

Chinese Proverb

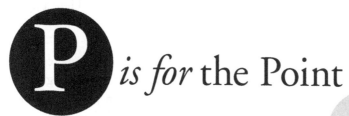

is for the Point

What is it,
by the way?

Insight for you

Now this is another belter. Mixing this principle in with a dash of the others we've already considered, this *really* makes the difference that makes the difference for you being understood; being recognised and rewarded in your business, your office, your industry, your market.

We've all sat in meetings, in presentations, at lunches when someone has been rambling on or pontificating about something and we've asked ourselves 'what's your point?' or 'I wonder what the point is here?' Well if we're wondering that, so is everyone else – *if*, indeed, they're still listening.

Often, when I'm working with groups and especially with VIP clients when we're working one-to-one together, I'll ask a question and they'll explain and tell me the story – too much of the story. They can end up confusing themselves or, often, forgetting what my question was. In the fast-paced world in which we live, now more so than ever, they also start to lose the audience's attention. Now, the story *is* useful. Of course it is. There are keys and clues in there for us to listen out for and to start to get the meaning from. I often ask someone, especially when I can tell they've lost themselves 'so tell me, what's your point – in *one* sentence, please.' Now, your tone here is important (see T for Tone). People can tell I'm pressing them for a helpful reason from my tone – I don't say it in an accusatory way;

one that closes them down or puts them on the defence. Here a light, curious tone is important.

It's such a powerful question with the key part being 'in one sentence please.' It enables people to grab, from all the stuff swimming about in their head, the point. They always know it when *pressed* like that and it's a relief. They say 'well, I suppose it's XYZ' or 'gosh, one sentence? Well, it's XYZ.' That's when we get what the point actually is, with no frills, no explanation or justification. We help people access what they're trying to get across. Ah, now we have it. *Now* we can start to line up and sort – like a computer does – for what's going on.

The *point* here is, we need to get our point across. Especially as we work where so much rides on us being understood clearly, where decisions are made quickly and our credibility and effectiveness is constantly on show. We need our point to be clear and to land where we want it.

'If the fire alarm goes off, if the phone rings, if someone comes in and interrupts you, will people know what the point was of what you were saying?' I ask my clients this when they give too much story, too much detail and either lose – or never get to – *the point*.

As we've touched on in M for Meaning – sometimes it's useful for us to leave others to draw their own conclusions. Most of the time though, it's important for us to ensure people understand 'the point' we want to make; the nub, the core, the essence of what we're saying. You, like me, like to understand 'the point' – the 'why' we're doing this, listening to this, acting on this, planning for this, the 'what's this all about.' So here's how you can make sure you give people the point too, quickly, effectively and easily.

I want to introduce you to two models I use all the time. They help me as I get my point across, and they help my clients. Working with these models in large groups is really powerful. You can hear whoops of laughter and as many cries of frustration too as people try to hone their point down.

Firstly; the *PEP Model*. This one is easy, conversational in style and simple to remember.

Point +
Explanation/detail x 3 (*3 points are important*)
Point (again)

Ask yourself 'what's my point?' You'll know. You already know. If you had to jump out of a plane with a parachute and the last person you spoke to before you jumped asked you 'what's the point?' about your subject; you'd know. I promise.

In a similar way, one of our friends chose the name of her daughter; (my goddaughter Beatrice), from the other names swimming around in her head when I asked her if she had to jump from a plane and choose her baby's name just before she did, which one would she choose? She chose the name *Beatrice* immediately and intuitively before she *metaphorically* had to jump out of the plane. Beatrice has really grown into her name and our friend Karen still remembers how she decided on it.

OK, so you've got your point. With this PEP formula you get your point across without putting too much story in and without taking too much time and energy to get it across.

Point: 'It's important for us to have a holiday in June' for example.

E for Explanation.
1. We'll have a change of scenery and be able to catch up.
2. It's a great time of the year in our diaries to get away.
3. It's been 6 months since we've been away together.

Point: 'Yes, it's important for us to get away together in June.'

I told you what my point is; that I think it's important to have a holiday in June. I supported *why* I believe it's important for us and I repeated and reiterated, *the point*.

P	Point
E	Supporting Point 1 Supporting Point 2 Supporting Point 3
P	Point

This is such a useful tip for you to use to help you to be understood and an easy one to remember. If you look at the letter E it has 3 horizontal lines leading from it, so the E for Explanation is where you give 3 (not 4 or 10) 3 *brief* explanation points to support your point. Brief is the key word here. People can always *ask you* for more information *if* they need it but if you get out your point followed by your 3 supporting points, *then* reiterate your overall point; it's out there. It's clear for people. You come across as someone who knows. They're left with your point.

Three is the magical number here. One isn't enough, six is too many. Three supporting points gives your listener/reader enough to start with. You can even say 'one it's X, two it's Y and three it's about Z.' It's conversational and people like to hear you lay out your supporting points for them.

You can use this setting out emails; planning a phone call; a presentation; a speech.

'What's your point Kay?' Good question.

When you get your point across quickly and concisely, people will respect you for it.

1. They'll understand where you're coming from.
2. They'll get a sense of what they need to be thinking about.
3. You'll save yourself precious time and energy.

So, it's really worth getting your point across quickly and concisely because people will respect you for it. They'll also *wonder* how you're doing it. Aha.

Another helpful – and easy – way to remember how to get your point out and how to support it is by having an image of an inverted pyramid in your mind. I first read about this in a great little book called *The Unwritten Laws of Business* by W. J. King.

The idea is to think about how you get your point across like a pyramid on its head.

More details (as required)

Detail

Point

Let's start here and work upwards

Can you see, you get your point out first, up front. Build up the information as go along but get your point out quickly.

Know that from here, you then add more, as – *and if* – required. Your point is out first; people know what you're thinking about. In the book it tells us 'the trick is to convey the maximum significant information in the minimum time, a valuable asset to anyone.'

Ideas for you to work with today:

- Draw yourself the PEP model. Put the words by the side of it and pop it on a sticky note and stick it on your screen; the phone; your notepad. Take a few seconds to ask yourself – before picking up the phone, going to a meeting or starting an email – 'OK, what's my point? What 3 things support this point? Right, 1, 2 and 3. Now, let's put the point out again.' You'll find after using this a couple of times it becomes second nature for you, a habit. It's conversational, that's the beauty of it so you can map it out in your head and use it.

- Remember the picture and principle of the *inverted pyramid*. Notice how and where people around you start in relation to the pyramid and how they explain things to you (and *if* there's any structure to it). Most times, there won't be. You notice it when there is because it's so easy to get to grips with what the person's saying.

- Share these principles and models with your colleagues – and friends and family – so they can help you too, as they explain things to you!

Inspirations for you:

'If you be pungent, be brief; for it is with words as with sunbeams – the more they are condensed the deeper they burn.'
Robert Southey

'Any fool can make things bigger, more complex, and more violent. It takes a touch of genius – and a lot of courage – to move in the opposite direction.'
Albert Einstein

'Simplicity is the ultimate sophistication.'
Leonardo Da Vinci

It is not
the answer
that *enlightens,*
but
the question.

Decouvertes

Q *is for* Questions

Which type
to use, when
and why?

Insight for you:

I've hinted throughout the book about how important questions are.

Questions are a secret, powerful ingredient for connecting you to people, for helping you understand and then for helping you to be understood yourself.

You can sprinkle questions liberally throughout your conversations; everywhere in your life. Trust me, the quality of your information; guidance; insights and decisions rely mainly on the quality of *your* questions. Both the questions you ask the people around you *and* the questions you ask yourself.

Our questions are crucial to us digging deeper, connecting with people, understanding what's going on. This principle takes up a few more pages than other principles so bear with me and know that it's going to be worth it. Understanding and then choosing my questions more carefully has been – and still is – one of the quickest ways I've built relationships, found things out, connected with people, been appointed and learned so much – and still do.

For ease I'll separate the questions you have to play with into two sections.

- Firstly – Open questions.
- Secondly – Closed questions.

With each we'll explore the differences, and when to use which and why.

< < < O p e n > > > questions

Open questions I like to think of as a space you invite someone to step into. Think of a big landscape, a wide, open space and that's the effect of an open question. You ask an open question and your listener; your reader; your audience is invited to go within and search for information; for detail. From this detail you then choose whether you want more information. If you do, you bring out another of your open (or closed) questions. Here's how.

Open questions are great for networking events; for business meetings; for cocktail parties; people love being asked about themselves, they love it when you're interested in them, quizzical about them and I promise you, you get to lead the conversation – *if you want to* – with your questions. Now there's a thought. The person who asks the questions, leads the conversation.

The difference for you after reading this principle is that you'll be choosing *consciously* now between the open/closed questions you already use – but you're probably not *really* aware of how powerful the are. Certainly I wasn't until I learned about the differences and the power of them when first studying for my coaching qualifications. You'll be 'all over them', as we say, in just a few pages.

Now if you're thinking 'yes, yes Kay questioning and all that, I know about questions', I thought it will be useful to pop this quote in here from Rudyard Kipling, one of the great storytellers and poets of the late 19th and early 20th centuries.

'I keep six honest serving men: They taught me all I knew: Their names are *What* and *Why* and *When* and *How* and *Where* and *Who*.'

So, your open questions begin with What? When? How? Where? Who?

You'll notice I've left out 'Why' and you can skip to W to find out *why*. 'Why' is so important it has a chapter of its own. I've also left out 'Which' and you'll find out about that, too, as you read on.

So, asking open questions invites the person being asked the question to give you information; to go inside and search for information for you. Open questions also give you time to consider the information given to you; to consider your position; to notice what and indeed how the person is saying what they're saying *before* you decide to respond.

You buy yourself time because asking open questions makes the other person do the work. They give you information versus you either having to make assumptions or telling them what you think they think. Open questions also tell the other person you're interested in them.

Here's an example. A client wanted to know whether her business partner had decided to go ahead on a project or not. She said 'I don't want to be confrontational but I'm going to ask him, have you decided yet?' This is a closed question. More on this later but it's a *closed* question. Have you decided yet? i.e. the first answer that springs up in the mind is either 'yes' or 'no' i.e. *closed*.

Our brains automatically go off and search for the answer and unless you're aware how powerful questions are, you're automatically programmed to answer them.

So, after we discussed the differences together instead of asking 'Have you decided yet' she asked 'Where are you with your decision on XYZ project?' – now that's an open question. An open space for her partner to step into. 'Where are you with etc?' Her partner was invited to share a bit of information without the 'Yes or No' being the first answer he gave.

What's going on with your finances at the moment? *How* do you know that? *When* did you start reading this? *How* long have you been in business? *What* made you decide on your career? *How* long have you been married? *Where* did you two meet? *What's* your favourite past time? *What* do you particularly enjoy about it?

Now if you re-read those questions and run through the answers, as if we're chatting together, you'll notice how you go inside, search for information; and if you write your answers down they'll take space, they'll be more than yes/no. They have to be more than yes/no because they're open questions. Open for you to answer. Open for you to share. Open for you to give me some information.

Most people love to share information about themselves, their thoughts and decisions. Open questions will help you find out more of what you want to know and keep the conversations going and by asking them it also takes the spotlight off you and puts it on to the other person. Interesting. You then decide if you want to ask more questions. Some people call it 'drilling down' further. I prefer to think about it as more like being a sniffer dog. Finding out more.

I remember splashing about in a pool on holiday and chatting with a woman who told me how she felt panicky when she went to cocktail parties, saying, 'I never know what to tell people.' My immediate response, as I splashed about, was 'what about asking them questions then? Ask people lots of open questions. People actually don't *want* you to tell them all about yourself anyway.' She looked a bit surprised, especially as we had bobbed down towards the deep end and with me being 6ft tall I was still able to stand

and she suddenly was out of her depth both physically and, for a moment, mentally.

We discussed it and giving her these types of open questions and examples of how they work and why they work, it was as if the sun came out from behind a cloud for her. She went off to her beach bag and wrote them down to use.

Now in your workplace; you can already imagine how powerful it is to be able to choose *when* to ask for information, more information, or to ask for more input about a decision or a situation when you want it. It's also a simple way to relax yourself to ask open questions, you get to settle yourself if you're feeling unsettled or uncertain. Give the metaphorical spotlight and microphone to the other person.

Where? When? Who? How? What? Your big open space that you invite people to step into.

What about 'Which?' Well 'which' tends to take you into decision-mode and so is leading into the 'closed question' territory. Which one did you pick? Which do you prefer? Which do you want me to do first? Which is it to be, this one or that one?

Can you hear in your head that 'Which' starts to pin the other person down and that's OK, that's fine *if* it's what you want. If you want more information, more detail, if you want to buy more time, then keep your questions open in that 'open space'.

>>>Closed<<< questions

Do you understand this principle? Is this simple? Have you decided to think more about your questions now? Could you start today? Will you tell anyone else about them? Can you get how important Q for Questions is? Would you be able to notice open/closed questions now?

'Yes' is likely to be the answer to all of the above. Yes or no. They're all closed questions which request a decision, a position, a 'yes' or 'no' answer. It's as simple as that. If you want yes/no you ask a closed question. If the other person wants to be difficult, is anxious or is in a rush, they can just give you a 'yes' or 'no'. It is, after all, all you asked for.

It's not the *open space* of the open question, is it? No. I describe a closed question as a bit like a tunnel. You send people into a tunnel where yes or no is to be found. They *may* offer you more information after saying 'yes' or 'no', also, they may not. It's then up to you if you ask another question. Aha.

Closed questions are important when we want to hone in on a decision. When we need to know if something's happened, been decided on, been done. What's so key for you here, is that you know, understand and then use the difference as you go about your business; as you go off and find out from clients what's happening; as you ask your colleagues and friends about things. It's the difference that makes the difference and now you *know* the difference.

Here's a great example and I virtually shouted at the radio. A BBC reporter told us he'd interviewed a famous American actor about his recent film and what it was like filming in the English winter when he was used to Californian sunshine. 'Did you enjoy filming in London?' 'Were you happy to be here for an English winter?' 'Do you think there's a chance of a sequel?' 'Are you looking forward to seeing your family?'

You can hear how the actor could have just said 'yes' 'no' 'yes' 'yes'. He could have just stopped at that if he'd wanted to be difficult, if he wanted to close the conversation down. The reporter could have asked the same essence of these questions but invited the actor into a space for him to fill with 'What was it like filming in London?' 'How did you get on with our English winter?' 'What's the thinking about a sequel?' 'How's the family? What did they think about you being here?' Totally different, isn't it? Yes.

So to mix open and closed questions is the key here. Decide when you want a decision, a position, decide when you're ready to get commitment 'so will it be ready by Friday then?' after you've asked 'where are you with the report?' You don't have to pin people down to yes or no *straightaway*. If you do, then now you at least know that you are. Now you can choose.

Ideas for you to work with today:

- Remember your space or your tunnel. Notice today when you ask a closed question if you'd have preferred to ask an open one first.

- Listen to how you're asked questions by those around you. Notice how if you're asked a closed question, you could choose to answer just 'yes' or 'no'. To wake someone up, just answer, 'yes I have' or 'no I didn't' and notice their surprise. You can always carry on and fill out your answer a bit for them but notice the way the question doesn't ask you to open up, you have to *choose* to.

- When you prepare to approach someone to ask something, *think* about what you really want to know, understand or find out. Then work backwards with your questions. Some people call it 'reverse engineering'. Think what you want to find out and then work back to which questions to ask to help get you that information. Jot them down, while you're practicing, it helps to just jot your questions down, a bit like a map. I still sometimes jot down the questions I want to ask to get me to where I want to go.

Inspirations for you:

'It is better to know some of the questions than all of the answers.'
James Thurber

'Quality questions create a quality life. Successful people ask better questions, and as a result, they get better answers.'
Anthony Robbins

'My greatest strength as a consultant is to be ignorant and ask a few questions.'
Peter Drucker

" Never take a **person's dignity**: it is worth everything to them and **nothing to you.** "

Frank Barron

R *is for* Respect

A lesson from Bambi

Insight for you

'If you can't say anything nice; don't say nothin' at all.'

Now, even though the film Bambi was made nearly 70 years ago, and the character saying this was a rabbit called Thumper, a cute, wise sidekick to Bambi the film's hero, there's something in that phrase for all of us. Very much *something* in there for us. Especially as we go about our business.

Whilst Thumper's intention is good, it's also not realistic nor is it very helpful. Only saying 'nice' things turns us into at worst a sycophant, a flatterer, a toady and at best it means we're someone who never really expresses an opinion. Your opinion may not be what the other person wants to hear but – depending how you express it – it may be exactly what they *need* to hear. Honesty, insight, another perspective. The trick is to be respectful as you do so.

Mary Kay Ash, the hugely successful American entrepreneur who, in the 1980s, built an empire for women to enable them to be stay-at-home mums and entrepreneurs at the same time, famously said 'Everyone has an invisible sign hanging from their neck saying "Make me feel important." Never forget this message when working with people.' Now, Mary Kay's advice is more helpful for us here than Thumper's. 'Keep me whole, respect me, I'm important too.' That's what we all want from other people, so let's give it to them too.

As you know by now, it's always worth hopping over to my dictionary and thesaurus – two of my most valuable tools – to go and find the definition and alternatives for the word I'm thinking about. I encourage you to use these too.

Respect – 'to value, to show consideration for, politeness, courtesy, civility.' It's about respecting the other person, their position, and their feelings as well as – *not instead of* – your own.

We've all been there haven't we? Someone says something, writes something and our immediate reaction is 'idiot, of course it's not like that, it's like this' or 'what a chump, they haven't got a clue!' Well they have got a clue, just maybe not the *same* clues you have. They're not an idiot, they're just different and so are their experiences, insights, and so is their knowledge. Crucially, *too*, so is their style. Different to you and different to your style.

As we already know, style plays a big part, and the A to Q principles we've discussed so far go a long way to making up *your* style.

We've been regularly bouncing about how different we all are; how different people need different things from us to be able to take action and be able to help us on our way. Showing people respect, showing people both politeness and courtesy; well, that's an ingredient that will help you everywhere in your life. *Especially* at work where we are mixing with people, sitting next to people, expecting and expected to interact with people we wouldn't necessarily choose to.

If you decide to respect the other person's opinion, position or input, then your 'come from' or your 'angle of approach' will be more inclusive, more open and most important of all, more *respectful* of the other person or persons.

This respectful approach is essential in meetings, in one-to-ones, in presentations; it comes out in your emails, your voicemails and it certainly comes out when you're just chatting. 'No, that's completely wrong' or 'Oh no, you've missed the point' and 'Oh for heaven's sake, can't you understand?'

You can hear them can't you – disrespectful of the other person. Would you like to have responses like that? I doubt it, me neither.

What happens when you start off with 'Oh no, you've missed the point' is that the other person is immediately pushed back, irritated, upset, put down. Even more if other people are around to hear it. Why do that straight off the bat? It's only going to make your attempt at putting your point across that much harder, because the other person is on their back foot. They may nod at you and agree with you but, at a deep, visceral level, they will resist you and your opinion just as you crushed theirs. Others may also decide to stay quiet in case you do the same to them. Lose/lose.

Notice how different 'Oh, I can understand how you might think that and XYZ' or 'that's an interesting angle, I think XYZ' and 'there may be a bit of confusion here, let's see, I think XYZ.' It's respectful; it's easier to take on your opinion when you've put some respect for the other person and their position up at the front.

Respect – it's rooted in late Middle English from the Latin *respicere* 'to look back at, to regard.'

Well, if you 'look back at, or regard' your colleagues, clients, bosses with this attitude of accepting differences, accepting their position, their knowledge at the same time as putting across your own, then you'll always have an easier passage in the world. You'll still have your opinions and input, and they're still allowed to have theirs.

Ideas for you to work with today:

- Notice today when your reaction pops up with 'No' or 'that's not right' and instead of putting that out there first, pause for a second, and the first thing you might say is 'yes, I can understand how you might think that' or 'hmmm, that's interesting, tell me a bit about that.' Before disagreeing and putting what you think across, keep the other person 'whole'. Respect their position first and they'll find it easier to take on yours.

- When you do take that moment and respect the other person's position, notice their reaction. You'll notice your own too; more ease, less friction. Less friction is good for everyone. Especially you.

- Today, particularly, have your radar programmed to notice how other people (or *if* other people) respect each other. You'll notice this when commuting, in coffee shops, in the office, in the street. There's energy, an attractive energy, about you when you're more open and more respectful of other people and how they are, what's going on with them. Allowing people to go first; holding the door for them; moving to let them in/on (so many times people pretend to ignore each other and it just doesn't help anyone). You'll notice this in other people now you're really looking for it, and you'll notice it in yourself.

Inspirations for you:

'I'm not concerned with your liking or disliking me. All I ask is that you respect me as a human being.'
Jackie Robinson

'We confide in our strength, without boasting of it, we respect that of others, without fearing it.'
Thomas Jefferson

'Respect for ourselves guides our morals; respect for others guides our manners.'
Laurence Sterne

If **history** were taught in the form of stories, it would **never** be forgotten.

Rudyard Kipling

S *is for* Stories

Once upon a time...

Insight for you

Choosing 'S is for Stories' is to remind us of the importance our stories play in our lives.

We tell stories to each other all the time, we explain our experiences in stories – 'Well, I'd just set off for the station, popped my earphones in to listen to the radio, bundled myself up in my coat and scarf, when a car drew up alongside me. I quickened my step, as I wanted to be on time today and by the way, who speaks to strangers in cars anyway? Again, the car stopped a little way ahead of me and the window went down and a voice suddenly said, "well you haven't changed, have you Kay?" It was such a shock.'

This is a quick story about an old friend of mine and I just hadn't seen him for about five years as he'd been living abroad. He'd spotted me in the street and was trying to offer me a lift to work. It's immediately engaging because I set it out as a story. If I had said to you 'a friend of mine stopped me in the street and offered me a lift' it would still be true but the difference is huge. I'm setting out facts and leaving out the story. It's less engaging; it doesn't draw you in, not in the same way.

We have our own story about how we got to be who, where and how we are – we live it and tell it to people all the time and how we tell it to people plays a large part in how engaging we are. If I say to you 'well, my parents were called Philip and Mary and they met when they were in their twenties and got married and decided to have children' that's firstly all true and factual, and secondly and, more importantly, dull.

'Well, my parents were called Philip and Mary and they met when my Mum decided the chap playing tennis near her house was 'the one' for her. Her dog, Wag, had never had so much exercise. Mum would drag Wag out of his bed, whether he wanted to come or not, and take him for a walk to be 'innocently' walking past the tennis courts every day whilst Dad (*he didn't know he was to be my Dad then of course*) was playing tennis. 'Oh, hello, I've noticed you walking your dog here, what's his name?' Dad asked one day when he left the court, as Mum innocently walked by dragging poor Wag with her. They were married within 2 years.'

Which is more engaging? Which version took you on a bit of a journey? Which version has a message in there? We both know, of course, that the second version, the story, is the one that captures our imagination.

There's a hint of tenacity and humour on my mum's part, long-suffering and canine faithfulness on Wag's part and innocence and surprise on my Dad's. There's a lesson in there too – going for something or someone you want, it doesn't have to be head on, it can be in a subtle 'oh, fancy seeing you here' kind of way. Use the resources you have around you – Wag, the proximity, timing coupled with my Mum's tenacity.

What's my point? (*I know, P for Point*). Well my point here is that telling stories engages people and teaches lessons – often under the radar – as they capture imagination and help people understand. They also draw people to you and help you get a message or your point of view across in a way that keeps others interested.

When I work with clients – both groups and individual clients – we are always looking for stories to be able to use to convey a message. There are some key questions to ask yourself which helps pull out a story to use. One of these is 'if you had to compare your message to something you've done in life, what's it like?' It's called an *analogy* – 'a comparison between two things, typically on the basis of their structure and for the purpose of explanation or clarification.'

If you're preparing a presentation, always look for a couple of stories to use to 'transport' the message, the point of your presentation. We think about the audience, what's going on with them and what they know and want to know, and then find a story that either you have or that we know about and use this to help map across the point.

It engages the listener, the reader. Using stories to describe a message, to help people understand is one of the most time-tested ways of engaging others. Cave dwellers used the pictures that we still find on cave walls to tell stories before language was used. Think how as children we loved being told stories 'read me a story' 'tell me a story please' – if you have children they probably ask you that now and remembering being a child, you'll have loved hearing, reading and learning stories. Why stop? In truth, if you think about it, we still love being told a story. Think about the films we go to see, the books we read, television programmes we watch. More often than not we'll be following a story.

I know I keep saying 'engaging' but the word is just exactly what I want you to grab and hold in your mind – and if you can't *engage* people, connect, make people listen to you, 'get' what you're saying, then you're always going to be behind those people who can. Those people tell stories and use stories to help them grab, keep and engage others' attention.

There's a model here I want to share with you to help you as you flex your story-telling muscles. It's a bit of a hybrid I've made up from something I learned in Daniel Pink's book *A Whole New Mind* and popped in an ingredient I add of my own.

The essence of telling a story, which engages and inspires is to use the DIOR formula – a bit of designer *couture* for you in fact. Daniel Pink's formula has the letters DIR and you'll notice why the O makes a difference.

D is for Departure. What happened, what was happening that makes the story pertinent, relevant? What was the struggle at the time and what brought it to a head? Who else was involved and what was happening with them?

I is for Initiation. What happened that changed this? Perhaps a new skill was learned, a change of circumstances and a new introduction to someone or something. Something happens to start the change.

O is for Ongoing. This added ingredient is where we show what was happening *whilst* this initiation happened.

R is for Return. Here is where the new beginning or the outcome, learning, is found and here's where the point of your story is brought out.

A bit like the PEP model in P for Point – you can use this to practice telling more stories. And just like the PEP model, keeping attention is to keep it simple, keep on point. Too much detail and your listener/reader starts to disengage, lose interest and your message gets lost.

Let's use mum and dad's story just to show you how the DIOR model works.

Departure: 'Well, my parents were called Philip and Mary and they met when my Mum decided the chap playing tennis near her house was 'the one' for her.

Initiation: Her dog, Wag, had never had so much exercise. Mum decided that walking Wag was the way to keep seeing that chap playing tennis. One day he'd notice her.

Ongoing: Mum would drag him out of his bed, whether he wanted to come or not, and take him for a walk – whatever the weather – to be 'innocently' walking past the tennis courts every day whilst Dad (he didn't know he was to be my Dad then of course) was playing tennis.

Return: 'Oh, hello, I've noticed you walking your dog here, what's his name?' Dad asked one day when he left the court as Mum innocently walked past with poor Wag. They were married within 2 years.'

Now, the 40+ years of marriage – highs and lows – which followed, well that's another story. It's so powerful to include stories in your day-to-day conversations. You can boil them down really effectively using this model. Remember, we all want to keep attention and keep the point clear so having the structure really helps.

Ideas for you to work with today:

- Listen out for good stories that go past you. You'll hear them on the radio, on the TV and read them in the newspaper. Notice them and notice how they carry you, the effect they have on you. Store them in your story bank. I have a note pad and jot down a couple of words to prompt me when I hear a good story. They're gold for you to use.

- Take the DIOR model and fit the flow of a story you have or one you've picked up into the model and then practice. Just as with the PEP model in P, you have to break things down and fit them in to the model and then you find the flow. Like all things; it takes a bit of practice before it becomes natural.

- If you have children or grandchildren, or in my case – god-children – flex your story-telling muscle by telling freestyle stories rather than reading from a book. Think about a lesson you want them to have, something that will help them and then use the DIOR model to slot the pieces in. You can just start with the D and then make the IOR part fit in as you go on – they won't know will they? It's your story, isn't it, and they don't know how it unfolds anyway.

Inspirations for you:

'If you want a happy ending, that depends, of course, on where you stop your story.'
Orson Welles

'Why was Solomon recognized as the wisest man in the world? Because he knew more stories (proverbs) than anyone else. Scratch the surface in a typical boardroom and we're all just cavemen with briefcases, hungry for a wise person to tell us stories.'
Alan Kay

'Life itself is the most wonderful fairytale of all.'
Hans Christian Andersen

"Don't look at me in that tone of voice."

David Farber

T *is for* Tone

TONE,
Tone,
tone

Insight for you

DO YOU UNDERSTAND? Now, you can tell from this that I'm *shouting* because in these days of more and more verbal interactions being replaced by written – email/texting/chat/web pages – there has to be a way of expressing the tone of what we're saying. Lots of little ditties like showing smiley faces, winks etc are put in to effectively lighten the tone of messages. Know what I mean? ;-)

Personally, I hate reading capital letters – they're actually more difficult to read (we scan words naturally and when the words are a sea of capitals, they're difficult to scan) and reading them feels as if the writer is SHOUTING.

The *tone* of things is important – the tone you choose to express the words you say.

The tone you use in your voice, when you speak – just as when you write – is a much more significant piece of being understood than people think.

In 1970 a book entitled *Kinesics and Context* by Ray Birdwhistell was published. The author, an American anthropologist, put forward the theory that inter-personal communication uses all the senses and that when broken down 7% of our success as we communicate comes from the words we use – and the other 93%? Well 55% from our physiology – how we stand, breathe, smile, how we hold our shoulders, our posture. The remaining 38% is tonality. The tone of our voice.

Now you may choose to believe this or you may not. I certainly believe that the words we use and how we use them play a much bigger part than just 7%. Especially now when so many of our conversations are written down and happen electronically.

Choosing T for tone in this book is to put to you just how important it is to think about, and be aware of, your tone of voice and the tone of your messages.

Your voice plays a big part in how people respond to you. The physical part of our voice, the way we speak, is largely learned – who influenced us as we were growing up, the types of voices we learned to speak from. As we grow up, we are continually influenced by the voices we hear around us and, the good news is that – if you want to – there's a lot you can do to make your voice more effective for you. A voice coach will work with you on your breathing, pacing, where you speak from (your chest or your stomach, for example) and you can improve your delivery quickly with just a few exercises and a bit of practice.

Growing up I had elocution lessons – at the time I was very unimpressed 'why do I have to go to elocution?' I'd whine but mum wanted me to have the opportunity of learning how to pace, how to project and how to 'round off' my voice. I even won a competition reciting a poem about a cat on a wall – woo hoo. Since first studying NLP (Neuro-Linguistic Programming) I realise now *just* how important tone and tonality is. So, when I start working with clients I can quickly get a sense of how successful they are at engaging people and compelling people to action simply from their tone of voice. Let alone what they're saying.

You only have to see this simple exercise below to get just how easy it is to change the sense of a sentence with your tone.

Each word, when it's emphasised (even saying them in your head with the emphasis on the **bold** word) changes the sense of each sentence.

I want to learn how to use my voice more effectively.
(*neutral*)

I want to learn how to use my voice more effectively.
(*me, not you*)

I **want** to learn how to use my voice more effectively.
(*yes I do*)

I want to **learn** how to use my voice more effectively.
(*to study*)

I want to learn **how** to use my voice more effectively.
(*what to do*)

I want to learn how to **use** my voice more effectively.
(*put it to use*)

I want to learn how to use **my** voice more effectively.
(*not yours, mine*)

I want to learn how to use my **voice** more effectively.
(*specific part*)

I want to learn how to use my voice **more** effectively.
(*more than I am*)

I want to learn how to use my voice more **effectively.**
(*not ineffectively*)

I want to learn how to use my voice more **effectively?**
(*do I, am I sure?*)

This simple exercise is an easy reference to keep in mind as you mark-out; literally you're *marking out* the sense in the sentence with your tone, you're marking the meaning you want to get across. You're doing it anyway, all the time; the point here is to be more aware of how powerful it is. Then, as with everything you're now more aware of, you get to *choose* how you use your voice, your tonality.

It's so powerful when you really decide to pay attention to your tone. You can say all sorts of things to people and even though your words might not be what they want to hear, the message gets carried via your tone. People are sometimes shocked at what I'm able to say and get away with and I know that so much of this secret is about the tone I use and my physiology (smiling, eyebrows raised, breathing, head up, shoulders back).

Your tone comes across the minute you say 'Hello!' 'Hello?' 'Oh, hello' and you've put it out there how you're feeling (it may not be how you're feeling at all *but* the other person has started to – unconsciously – decide that's how you feel).

This is why when we hear a presenter say 'I feel great, it's wonderful to be here with you today and we're going to have fun' and their shoulders are slumped, their hands clenched tight, their eyes staring like a rabbit in the headlamps *and* their tone is tight and forced with no energy behind it. Do you believe them? Of course you don't. Are you looking forward to spending time with them? I doubt it.

Just as with F for feedback – putting the words together in a way that make them positive and helpful and then putting them across to the person with good posture and eye contact, an open and friendly expression, *plus* a tone of voice that has energy and positivity to it is a formula for successfully engaging people.

To get you much clearer on this (as you can imagine, this subject is too huge a piece to lay out fully in just a section here) I suggest you go and read up on it further. As you know, this book is about *principles* to mix together and I picked the Tone part because, as mentioned before, we use writing more than ever now to carry our message and our *tone* comes across, even though we're not in the room. Readers are saying it to themselves of course, as they absorb *what* and *how* you write and they can 'hear' you as they read your message in their voice, in their head – they can hear the tone of your message. What do you want them to hear?

What you'll find in 'Y is for Yours Truly' – that's a key piece to add in to your engaging tone of voice whether you're saying it or writing it.

Ideas for you to work with today:

- Notice and think about your own tone of voice today. Does your voice seem to come from your chest (this tends to make us sound higher and more breathless) or does your voice come from your stomach (this gives us a deeper tone and, by virtue of where it's coming from, you speak slower too). I can tell when I'm rushing along; then I consciously *put* my voice into my stomach, breathe into my stomach and it immediately slows me down, making, I believe, listening to me a more pleasant experience.

- Think about *where* your voice is coming from – high up in your chest or lower down in your stomach? Practice switching them around to understand the difference. Rather than sounding like a comedy act I'm suggesting that you become much more aware of *how* you sound and also where you emphasise your words. It's just as we discussed in 'A for Attitude'. If you think about what your angle of approach is as you write to someone, as you speak to someone, so you will adapt your tone of voice. Irritation, interest, concern, excitement, anger, fun – they all come out in your tonality so now start to become aware firstly of your own and then other people's. Notice their tone, where they're breathing from and, most importantly, notice the effect it has on you and others. We know this sub-consciously, but here it's about noticing the effect consciously, because then you can do something about it.

- Oh – and depending on *your* tone and angle of approach – now you understand more clearly the effect and the way to modify tonality and just how important it is, you can now also help others. If you've noticed their tone could be tweaked to help them get their message across more comfortably, play back to them what they said and how it sounded, because, more often than not people are completely unaware of the effects of their own tonality. Go on, I dare you. It might just be the difference that makes all the difference to them.

Inspirations for you:

'We often refuse to accept an idea merely because the tone of voice in which it has been expressed is unsympathetic to us.'

Friedrich Nietzsche

'All feelings have their peculiar tone of voice, gestures and looks, and this harmony, as it is good or bad, pleasant or unpleasant, makes people agreeable or disagreeable.'

Francoise de la Rochefoucald

'The quietness of his tone italicized the malice of his reply.'

Truman Capote

"Understanding is a **two-way** street."

Eleanor Roosevelt

U *is for* Understanding

Your
'Check-in'
Desk

Insight for you

Checking in with people – and often
with yourself – is so often overlooked
and undervalued.

'Well, I told them that I wanted XYZ and now look what's happened?' or 'It's so obvious what's happened.' Is it? How do you know it's so obvious? Did you check in?

When we know what we want to have happen, what we want done, what the next move should be, it's so easy to assume (remember the *'It makes an Ass out of U and Me'* – see G) everyone else does.

We say what we want, maybe bash out an email and hit 'send' with the full story in our mind and often only the headlines in the email. Or, I hear clients who say – often affronted 'well I told him what I wanted and I'm still waiting.' My response is always 'how do you know they know what you want?' 'How do I know? Because I told them.' Aha.

This is such a simple and effective principle to remember – I know because when I learned it, really learned it as opposed to skim-reading it and hitting and missing with it – you save yourself so much of our three most precious resources; time, money and energy, *and* avoid the frustration of mopping up misunderstandings.

When we say what we want, what the next move is, when we ask for something, it's very easy to just assume it's clear. It's also easy for the other person to assume it's clear too. The difference here is checking-in with them, with the people in your meeting, with the person on the end of the phone to hear *from them* what will happen now, what they think you've said, and *if* what you said made sense to them.

This has a double-edged bonus for you. Firstly, as you check-in for understanding so, at the same time, you check-in for commitment too. In Dr Robert Cialdini's book *'Influence, The Science of Persuasion'* (see H for How) he lays out for us how commitment and consistency are huge influencers – people want to follow through on what *they've* said and what they've done before. Trust me, now I know exactly how this works after a lot of trial and error, I use it every single day. I make sure my message has landed in the way I want it to and that the person on the other end of it has committed to doing what *they* say they will – and when.

OK, so having grabbed your attention for the 'why' part – why it's important, now let's think about the 'how.' How you do the check-ing-in without being patronizing or worse, sounding like a Woodpecker drumming away? You ask the other person what they've heard, what they've understood and you ask it in a way that makes it more about *helping you*, more about you understanding whether *you've* been clear. *Not* – which is so many people's approach – *not* in a way that implies you think they're an idiot and haven't got it.

So, the easiest expression and one I ask all the time is 'OK, so can you just tell me what will happen now please?' Then you wait. Wait. No more speaking or helping them. You wait. 'What will happen now please?' You're sending the other person a message to go inside and process what they've heard or understood and then to regurgitate it to you in a way that shows you *how* and *what* they'll do next. Because they're saying it (not just nodding or saying 'yes' to what you're saying) they own it, and – as you know – when you've said something, when you've committed to doing something, you own it and you're far more likely to follow through and act on it. Aha.

'Just so I've understood where we are, can you run past me what happens now please?' – it's another way of saying the same thing we've just said. Asking it in *this* way makes it about us and not the other person, it implies *we* need to understand and, again, it's not about the other person. It is, of course, about you checking both their understanding and their commitment but what you also find is that as they play it back to you, you *may* have been less clear or missed out something important – it works both ways.

This principle of your Check-In Desk applies not only to the outset of getting your message clear; it also applies when you're following up on things. I wanted to pop this in here for you because – whilst we have 'K is for Keep in Touch', it's so important for you, I'm going to re-position it here too. Also, this principle is more about gaining commitment as you check in. Other people's commitment is crucial for you to succeed.

When you want to know what's happening, where things are at, when something's going to be ready – instead of phoning or emailing and asking just that, you can adopt the same approach. This avoids the Woodpecker way – 'is it done yet?' 'When will it be ready?' 'What's happening?' – which often switches people off or they avoid telling you or responding to you.

Instead, using your Check-In Desk approach, tell them what's happening your side so they get to understand how the piece they own fits in. For example – you're waiting for some figures from someone, which will go into a report you're working on for a client.

'Hey there, just to let you know we've nearly finished the rest of the report, so knowing you're getting the figures for us for later today, I'll make an appointment to take it our client tomorrow for sign off. Great stuff.' Then wait.

Can you get all the implied outcomes, next moves, all the assumptions you're making and telling the person you're making about what's happening and what's going to happen? You're also showing them where their part fits in to a bigger scenario. It's really powerful. It then becomes about a wider set of people and circumstances and not just you wanting some figures. The 'are your figures ready then?' is implied and it's then up to the other person to give you their position about the figures. That's what comes out as you wait, having finished with updating them. Wait.

'Morning Bob, thanks for agreeing that the report will be finished by Friday morning. We've got the couriers lined up to take it to the printers so it sounds we're all on track. What do you think?' Then you wait. This is where *Bob* will tell you where he's at, or start to flag an issue. You've mapped out for him what's happening and what you know he's already agreed. You've reminded him what you understand will happen. It's then for him to come back with his position – or, from what my clients tell me, for him to say 'yes' and then jump off the phone and into action.

What I really want you to pick up here is that you haven't asked one of those closed questions which doesn't leave much room for manoevre, 'is it finished yet?' or 'Will it be ready by Friday?' Instead, you've made it broader and it's assumed that all's going well and you've also made a space for them to recommit or flag an issue about the next moves without, as Snowy says 'banging on' about what you want.

Ideas for you to start working with today:

- Think of something you're either waiting for or that you know is dependent on someone else's input. Think about *how* you agreed what the next move would be and ask yourself if you are 100% clear that whoever it is *knows* what you want? If you are, great. If not, get in touch with them and say, along the lines before, 'just so I'm clear about the next move, or what will happen now, can you remind me where we are please?' It's always about *you* needing to be clearer – not them.

- As you're finishing a phone call or signing off an email, remember to check in for commitment 'can you just tell me what will happen now please?' Then *wait* for the response – especially if you're on the phone. Wait.

- Notice how – and *if* – people check for your commitment or understanding. Notice if they 'tell' you what they understand will be happening next or if they actually ask you. There's a big difference in what happens to you inside, so notice it. If they ask you to say it back to them then notice how you become more committed than if they reel off what they understand you'll do next. Just notice it because it works both ways.

Inspirations for you:

'Unless commitment is made, there are only promises and hopes; but no plans.'
Peter Drucker

'Great organizations demand a high level of commitment by the people involved.'
Bill Gates

'All truths are easy to understand once they are discovered; the point is to discover them.'
Galileo Galilei

"Words are the voice of the heart."

Confucius

V *is for* Verbal

Make
your words
count

Insight for you

In T for Tone, we explored the findings of '*Kinesics and Context*' by Ray Birdwhistell, who puts forward that

> 38% of success at communicating is tone, 55% is physiology and 7% the words. Only 7%?

To do this book and Ray Birdwhistell justice, we must explore both the physiology *and* verbal piece. V for Verbal fits here in our A to Z and I always knew we'd include physiology here.

Let's think about physiology first. We touched on it in T for tone but it's such a big piece it's worth re-visiting here too.

When you meet someone for the first time, you extend your hand to shake theirs and say, for example, 'Hello there John, great to meet you. I've heard a lot about you.' If you say this to John with your eyes cast down, your shoulders slumped, your smile either fixed or non-existent and your extended hand like a dead fish, well good luck. John is going to know, before you've even *said* anything, that your words and your overall message don't match.

Now I'm not suggesting that you behave like Tigger from *Winnie the Pooh*, and bounce forward, slapping John on the back (opposite message and often overwhelming when you're first meeting someone). No, I'm putting it to you that before you've even opened your mouth, John has a sense of you. Notice the word *sense*.

John's eyes will be taking in how you look – both how you look at him and how you look physically – your dress and your posture; his ears taking in how you sound – the pitch and tone of your voice; his sense of touch with your handshake – the feel of you and the energy behind your handshake.

It's primal – our fight/flight mental awareness – designed from being the hunter and often the hunted. Whilst the methods of being the hunter and hunted are less overt at, say, a networking meeting (*you hope*) the essence of what goes on for us is the same.

We sum up (not always correctly I know, but we do it nevertheless) in seven seconds or less our first impression of that person. Sometimes – we all do it – we will try to avoid a person who's coming our way because of that first impression and often, if pressed, we'd say, 'I just knew what he'd be like.' Well we're mentally sorting with those fight/flight filters of ours all the time.

Physiology is a wide subject and too wide to fully explore here. Suffice to say, be really aware of your physiology and the effect it has on others. It's one of the key pieces for people being *mis*understood.

Are you smiling when you greet someone? Do you smile when you're speaking (depending on the subject, punctuating your conversation with smiles is, again, a huge piece of connecting with people – and it relaxes you. Remember we release serotonin – sometimes known as 'the happy hormone'. ;-)

Do you stand or sit up so that you look engaged and engaging, or are you slumped either in your chair or in your posture – as if the world's on your shoulders? Do you give someone's hand a gentle squeeze (not a vice-like grip by the way – another message completely) or are you handing them the limp fish? I'm posing these quick fire questions to you here to remind you and encourage you to notice both your own physiology and to notice that of those around you – what you like about it and what turns you off or makes you move away. It will stand out for you as you start to pay attention to it.

So, after physiology and tonality comes the verbal piece. The actual words you use and avoid. Again, this is too big a piece to fully explore in this section, and context is everything; *but* we've already talked about the importance of clear language, of engaging language, of positive (as opposed to negative) language. Helping people by telling them what we *want* and not what we *don't* want. Planting positive suggestions and ideas with your language.

We've thought about words to avoid or be wary of (no) and words to watch out for (but) and those to use more than you might have before (thank you). Putting some fun into your language, and weaving stories through your conversations, presentations, blend all these together to make your verbal piece more engaging, more compelling, more attractive to people.

As you already know, one of the most helpful things I do which gives me a broader range of words, more insight to the meanings behind the words and potentially better words for the situation is to use my Thesaurus and Dictionary on my computer. Right-click on the mouse of most computers and up come your options for these two.

Also, I'm always using the 'You' versus the 'I' principle we thought about and thinking about what engages other people, what's in it for them, what they're interested in. 'Who cares? So What? What's in it for me?'

What's in it for you is to be understood in a way you want to be, and in a way that changes *everything* – changes your level of success, your earnings, how people *get* you, how you feel about them and they about you – and how you feel about yourself.

Ideas for you to work with today:

● Think about the words you use and the way you use them. Have your dictionary and thesaurus closer to hand than normal and try and test yourself with them. Notice the words other people use to describe things and notice the effect they have on you.

● Be conscious about your posture and physical energy – how much gusto and energy you put into your voice, how you reach out to shake someone's hand, how they take yours, and really take note. As you do, you'll be learning just how much information there is in every moment, which often goes under our radar. Not anymore!

● Write down 5 words you want to use more and 5 words you want to avoid. Have them in front of you, consciously use / avoid them and as you do, notice the different energy that comes to you from the words. As we've said before, no need to be a fire-hose here. Do it gradually. By the way, someone I'm very fond of says that 'every day's a school day' and I also believe that's true and it's also true that a learning machine is an earning machine.

Quick, inspired action for you:

To add a real boost to your range of powerful, positive and inspiring words to use, you'll find a supplement to this book waiting for you at www.wayforwardsolutions.com – *Words that Work from A to Z*.

This free supplement is a collection of over 1,200 persuasive, inspiring, positive and motivational words for you to use in your conversations, your emails, your presentations, marketing, in your voicemails and – of course – to weave in to your messages as powerfully in your personal life as in your professional life.

They'll inspire *you* as you use them and motivate and energise, compel and encourage those who hear or read them as you use them.

Words that Work from A to Z will help you remind yourself of how powerful the language you use to express yourself is as you write, speak, persuade, inspire, compel and tell your stories, everywhere.

Go and get them, start working with them and tell me how they work for you at **support@wayforwardsolutions.com**.

Inspirations for you:

'Many a treasure besides Ali Baba's is unlocked with a verbal key'
Henry Van Dyke

'Words have the power to both destroy and heal. When words are both true and kind, they can change our world.'
Buddha

'Use of non-verbal communication to *soften* the hard-line position of others:

s = smile

o = open posture

f = forward lean

t = touch/tone

e = eye contact

n = nod'
Unknown

'Why?' is discouraged since it often implies criticism and evokes defensiveness.

Sir John Whitmore

W *is for* Why?

And *why* it can trip you up

Insight for you

If you've already read 'Q for Questions' then you'll remember we were going to explore 'Why' and the power of the word later in the book. Well, let's explore it now.

> 'Why' is such a small and yet powerful word to notice, to understand and to be aware of as you use it. Really, why?

Well, it does two things very quickly, immediately in fact. Two things you want to avoid.

- One, it sends people straight to the word 'because' which is justifying their actions/decisions and

- Two, it closes down information-gathering in the request for the reason or explanation.

Questions are crucial to us digging deeper, connecting with people, understanding what's going on. They help us buy ourselves time, they help us to go wider as well as deeper into what's happening. Understanding why 'why' can trip you up is a powerful principle to know.

Let me explain the trick about 'why' – and the powerful effect it has on us and, more importantly, the powerful effect it has on those we ask the 'why' question to.

When children are growing up (and yes, *we* probably did it too) it's seen as quite cute when they first start to ask 'why?' and then you answer and then they ask 'why?' again and again and, often again. As you answer them – or as you were answered yourself most likely, you'll probably say 'because' and 'because' etc until eventually, often in despair, *'because I say so!'*

Day to day, we're constantly asking questions to find out what's happening, what progress is being made, how people are, what the situation is etc.

Notice the difference in this scenario. Imagine I was with you and asked you what you're up to this weekend? You tell me, for example, 'oh, I'm off shopping with friends and then on to the cinema.' Then I say 'Oh, why are you going to the cinema?' You'll say, 'because XYZ film's out and I want to see it.' It's an innocent enough question with, in this case, no further agenda. Yet, you've justified to me 'why' you're going to the cinema. *Because* – and then you've gone inside and thought about the *reason* you decided to go to the cinema.

If I ask you the same question but when you tell me you're off to the cinema with friends instead I say to you 'aah, what are you going to see?' or 'who are you going with?' These are much less on-the-spot questions. They seek *information* not *justification* and when we justify ourselves we're on the defensive; we're explaining the reasons rather than giving information, however innocent the scenario. It's also quite irritating to have to explain why – and here's why. *Because* we have to take a position and the question implies – however innocently – some judgment behind it.

Now here's the really powerful bit. Take this scenario to the workplace, or to a home life discussion about something that has some emotion attached to it, 'why did you do that?' 'Why haven't you done that?' 'Why are you going there?' You can feel it can't you? You're immediately putting the other person on the back foot; so they have to start defending their decision or their position.

Being on the back foot, defending a decision or position, I think of two people fencing with their face shields and white outfits on, foils and the ready and *en garde*. Defending their position.

It's one of the many small words that make a *big* difference in our day-to-day conversations and one that directly affects the reactions and responses we get. Working with clients from solo business owners to middle managers up to Boards of Directors of public corporations, we inevitably explore the effect of this word and they all have 'aha' moments with the power – of the word 'why?' The trick is you don't *know* until you know, do you?

Now, there's an add-on to this. When you are explaining something, when *you're* telling people about a decision or offering them information then 'why' is a great word for *you* to use.

'You may be wondering why I decided to do this? Well, because this happened, it seemed clear to me to do this.'

'If you're wondering why this is important, let me tell you. Because etc.'

'I asked myself "why does this always seem to cause an issue?" and you know what I found out? Because ABC does this, then it leads us on to doing XYZ.'

You're able to explain, very naturally, when you pose yourself the question 'why' you've done something or 'why' something happened. Your listeners or readers are often asking themselves that question anyway; 'why is this happening?' 'Why are we doing this?' so answer it for them by posing yourself the same question.

The trick is to remember that when you're asking for information, when you're exploring circumstances or options you want people and their minds to be open (and information-gathering) not on the back foot and adopting the *en garde* position. Now you know *why*.

Ideas for you to work with today:

- Try it out with someone as an experiment and get his or her feedback from the experience. They'll tell you *why* they prefer one question to the other, *because* you've asked for a bit more information as opposed to put them *en garde*.

- Notice how often 'why' pops into your head today. Notice how it takes you a second to re-ask the question with Who? What? Where? When? or 'tell me a bit more about that.' Then notice what you find out that you may not have done if the person was on their back foot, on the defence.

- Remember that this principle is just as powerful – if not more powerful – at home where we really want to get the best out of those around us (and for them to get the best out of us). Instead of the 'why did you do that?' when your child or partner or parent does or says something – use your questions as before to explore further; 'tell me a bit more' or 'hmm, that's interesting – what was that about then?' I guarantee you that cutting your *output* of 'why' so you avoid the short-circuit route to justification will increase the *input* you get from others, the engagement and feeling of connection you receive and that, most definitely, is a good thing.

Inspirations for you:

'A major stimulant to creative thinking is focused questions. There is something about a well-worded question that often penetrates to the heart of the matter and triggers new ideas and insights.'
Brian Tracy

'He who asks is a fool for five minutes, but he who does not ask remains a fool forever.'
Chinese Proverb

'Judge of a man by his questions rather than by his answers.'
Voltaire

"We must embrace pain and burn it as fuel for our journey."

Kenji Miyazawa

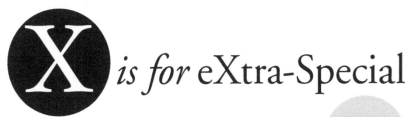

X *is for* eXtra-Special

Use your own *Secret Sauce*

Insight for you

A friend of mine asked recently 'What's your unfair advantage – and do you even know about it?'

The essence of this question is about turning lemons into lemonade. It's about looking for, thinking about, and then recognising your special edge/gift/angle. I call it your *Secret Sauce* – something you have or a learning you've acquired, normally as a result of something that's happened to you and it's what makes you who you are; your *Secret Sauce* makes you different in a way that helps you; that distinguishes you; that helps people to understand and connect with you. Often you don't even consciously know about it or acknowledge it.

Working with people who want to raise their visibility and influence as they work, this is one of the first places I start with them: 'What is it about you or what has happened in your life that you've struggled with?' The reason I ask this question is that it's often exactly these sorts of things that actually make us who we are and – if we recognise them – they become an 'unfair' advantage to us.

The interesting twist to this is that we often either overlook this *Secret Sauce* or even try to hide it. This is exactly what other people *want* to understand about us; it makes us real. Our struggles or our 'unfair' experiences make us stronger and people can connect to us more easily because of it. It makes us different and distinguishes us.

As soon as I read this question the first time, I knew what my 'unfair' advantage is.

Being 6ft tall since I was 14. Growing up, I was so often teased and asked 'what's the weather like up there Lurch?' and 'is there enough oxygen up there for you?' oh, and one of the best ones can *still* be 'Ooooh, aren't you tall?'

I'd often (*and still do*) say 'Oh, thank you for telling me, I hadn't noticed!' In my teens, I used to go to parties and immediately take my shoes off saying my feet hurt. In reality, I wanted to be shorter, to blend in more.

Now, I recognise – and leverage – that being tall means I'm noticed, I'm remembered. Often when growing up, I was assumed to be either older or wiser (or both) than I was. My height gives me a natural presence, which in business, just as in life, helps. I have no choice anyway; I was – and still am – 6ft and the choice was always how I deal with it – what I made it mean to me.

It would have been easy to have slouched, to have tried to hide it by wearing flat shoes all the time but actually, I really like being tall and I stand up straight with – as Mum used to say – 'shoulders back, chest out.' I also wear high heels as and when I want to. Oh, and I'm married to someone a fair bit shorter too. So what? It's all about perception and how you *perceive* your 'unfair' advantage, your *Secret Sauce*.

Snowy believes one of his unfair advantages is having a tall wife. He can 'find her in a crowd'. If you think about it, it also says a lot to other people about his own self-assurance and self-confidence.

Asking a few other people recently, just off the cuff, what they've struggled with and now could be their 'unfair' advantage. They've all been able to tell me what theirs is.

- **One friend** – 'Being Scottish – I'm remembered, I'm different and people like my accent.'

- **Another** – 'My dyslexia's made me be so much more creative.'

- **Snowy** – 'My dad dying when I was so young helped me know how to look after myself and appreciate how hard my Mum worked.'

- **A client** – 'Nearly dying of cancer when I was 16. It makes me realise what's really important and what's just 'noise' in my life.'

Being open, being real, being understood – they all go together. When someone tells you a bit (and I emphasise here, *a bit*) about his or her struggles, or the 'it wasn't always like this', we immediately warm to that person. It makes them human; *real* – even more so if they're seen as someone successful; the boss for example; or a well-known character. When we allow our *Secret Sauce* to come through, our vulnerability, our struggles, which have helped to make us who we are – other people connect to us much more quickly and naturally.

We all have a *Secret Sauce* and – like any special gift – it's ours to use and bring out to both help and inspire others, as well as to help and inspire ourselves.

What's yours and do you even know about it – yet?

Ideas for you to work with today:

- Think about your 'unfair' advantage. What is it that's shaped you and how do you allow it to positively influence your life? If it doesn't, how could it? What *could* you make it mean?

- A great way to find out if you don't instinctively know, is to ask 3 different people who know you well. Literally ask them 'what do you think is my unfair advantage' and just stop and listen to what they say. Often they'll all come up with the same thing, my friends all did. Others often see – and appreciate – things in us, or about us, that we don't.

- When you become clearer about this, recognise if and how you can *allow* it to be your Secret Sauce. It's a big part of communicating the person you really are, everywhere you are.

Inspirations for you:

'If you can find a path with no obstacles, it probably doesn't lead anywhere.'
Frank A. Clark

'One of the secrets of life is to make stepping stones out of stumbling blocks.'
Jack Penn

'You may not realise it when it happens, but a kick in the teeth may be the best thing in the world for you.'
Walt Disney

"My name may have buoyancy enough to float upon the sea of time."

Richard Watson Gilder

Y *is for* Yours Truly

The power
of your –
and their –
name

Insight for you

The power of using peoples' names;
the power of hearing your own name
when it's used; the way it immediately
engages and connects you; how it even
wakes you up.

When I learned that it's one of the most visceral experiences, one that we all crave, to be known and to *know* that we're known and to know that we're remembered by others, then it so easily made sense. The same day I read about the power and effect of using people's names – it was in Dale Carnegie's book *How to Win Friends and Influence People* – I immediately started to use everyone's names much more than I had before. It's almost magical and has now become a habit, something I just do.

It's also powerful to know that the fastest way to disconnect from someone – intentionally or otherwise – is to confuse their name, mispronounce their name and keep forgetting their name. It's a real turn off.

You know how easy it is to pontificate and chat away to people – in writing as well as face-to-face – and never *mention* their name? Well, the minute – or let's say, the second – you decide to start using everyone's name more, then you'll notice immediately how much more engaged people are with you; how you have their attention – sometimes despite them not wanting to give it to you. It tells them – and you – that you're thinking of them; it says that you actually know their name (so many people don't take any notice of your name and it's just that – *your* name, your identity). It tells them that you're engaging with them, that you're directing your message *to* them and *for* them and not generally blathering on.

It's a subtle, secret – and easy – ingredient to add to your conversations; your emails; your meetings; your networking; your cocktail parties – everything really. It works as effectively in writing as it does verbally and at work that same as at home.

Hearing your name – just as when someone hears his or hers – cuts through all the 'noise' of what's going on and goes straight in and grabs attention. The message the brain hears is 'oh, it's us, we're on. We'd better pay attention.' It's really powerful to *know* this.

Sometimes we forget the name of the person we've just been introduced to; we're mid-flow and then realise we've forgotten their name. If you make it your new habit to immediately say back their name to them as you're introduced 'well, nice to meet you Jane' or 'Jane, it's a pleasure meeting you' two things happen.

Firstly, you tell Jane you heard her name and have remembered it; your greeting is more meaningful to her because her name is included in there. Secondly, it helps you to 'engage brain' and remember her name. You can start avoiding those 'help, I've forgotten who I'm talking to' moments, which are both excruciating and also a reflection of our lack of attention towards that person. Whoops.

So, how do we start using someone's name comfortably? The word *comfortably* is important here. It's not about saying 'Oh yes, Jane, I agree Jane – and Jane what do you think about that Jane?' Of course it's not. That would be counter-productive; Jane would think you've either lost the plot or are over-the-top and to be avoided.

The way I find most comfortable and a great way to start, is to use a person's name when asking them a question or when asking for a response. 'So Jane, how long have you been working here?' or 'tell me a bit more about that, Jane, please.'

When you're writing – especially in emails – pop the person's name in a couple of times within the body of the message. It's obvious to *start* the message with the person's name, isn't it? I'm including it here because so many people *don't*. They just launch themselves at 'telling' the person what they want without even using their name; it's such a turn-off.

At the very least, start your messages with 'Hi Jane' or 'Dear Jane' or 'Jane, just to let you know' etc. You get the idea. I always ask clients 'Would you just burst into someone's office and launch straight off with what you want?' The answer is – usually – 'No, of course not.' You'd say something like 'Morning John, how's it going? Just to tell you etc.' Why would you start an email any differently – bursting onto someone's screen?

So, you've started with their name and now, within the content of the message, pop the person's name in at the end of a sentence; not *every* sentence, maybe every third or fourth. For example, 'Let me know which date works best for you, Jane' or 'How can we make this work for us both, Jane?' It's engaging, it's conversational and it's hard to ignore. Hard to ignore is a good thing. Being understood is about so many things and it's about being remembered and being noticed for the right reasons; it's not about being ignored.

Using people's names in a meeting is really powerful. Whether you're running the meeting or participating in it, when you come to comment – notice I've said *when* not if – or ask a question, use the person's name who has either just spoken or to whom you're directing your information. If you're running the meeting, instead of throwing out the question 'So what do you think of that?' use a few people's names. 'So what do you think about that, Jane?' and 'John, how will that work in your area?' What happens here is powerful to know. Both John and Jane are immediately engaged and involved – whether they want to be or not – *and* everyone else is suddenly aware that they might be asked a question too – they'd better pay attention as well.

One of my clients who worked with me on increasing her visibility towards getting a promotion said this was virtually magical or, as she put it, 'gob-smacking'.

You'll know from reading V (for Verbal) and T (for Tone) that it's very much about *how* you ask a question or how you throw the ball to someone. A conversational tone, a smile, raised eyebrows. Using people's name as well as these other principles is like putting the cherry, on the icing on the cake. Try it. The people whose names you use will immediately notice the difference; and so will you.

Ideas for you to work with today:

- When you greet people today, use their name. 'Hi there X' and 'Morning X, how's it going?' Notice yourself doing this and notice the response. Often it will be one of surprise. It really jolts the other person when they hear their name, especially when it's unexpected. Do this as you go into meetings; as you phone people; as you bump into people. It's so easy to just say 'Hi there' or 'Morning' without using the person's name. Engage with them and grab their attention quickly, by using their name.

- Notice yourself when you write an email – pop the person's name in there a few times. Certainly top and tail the email or note with their name. Why wouldn't you?

- When you're in a meeting today – or maybe having a meal (which, wherever you are in life, is a meeting of sorts, just with food) use people's names around the table. Again, not after every sentence but practice using their names more than you would normally do. You'll notice a difference in their response to you and so will they. You'll make them feel more connected, more important and regardless of their relationship to you, that's a good thing.

Inspirations for you:

'If names are not correct, language will not be in accordance with the truth of things.'
Confucius

'If you want to win friend, make it a point to remember them. If you remember my name, you pay me a subtle compliment; you indicate that I have made an impression on you. Remember my name and you add to my feeling of importance.'
Dale Carnegie

'And so with all things: names were vital and important.'
Algernon H Blackwood

It is a great thing to know the

season for speech and the season for silence.

Seneca (5 BC–65 AD)

is for Zip It

Wait.
Pause. Less
is More.

Insight for you

This is a tricky one for so many of us.
Wait. Pause. Think a bit.

Choose whether you're going to act; to respond. 'Zip It' is such a useful little phrase and it's easy to remember and to visualise.

It's so easy to assume we have to respond, to fire back. We receive a message, a phone call, an email and just respond, straight away. Either shooting from the lip or, when writing, shooting from the fingertip.

One of my clients described herself as so 'frustrated and high octane' when she first started working with me. As we began our work together on her becoming a more influential, comfortable communicator, she realized that her own 'shooting from the lip' style which resulted in her quick-fire responses to situations with her team, and sometimes with her family played a large part in how she was feeling. Fed up – to put it politely – and really frustrated.

As she began to think about things differently, trying new ways of getting her point over – or in her case – not communicating sometimes she realised that she had a choice as to when, *and indeed if,* she responded. This applied to people directly as they came to her, to situations, to emails or phone calls. As she started to think like this, everything started to change for the better. She coined for herself the great phrase 'masterful inactivity' which helps her – and now helps me and so many other people.

'Masterful inactivity' is *zipping it* in action, or really in chosen and considered *inaction*. I'm so proud of her; she grabbed information, ideas and insights from me as I listened and questioned her and then she immediately implemented them. In her case, implementing often meant waiting, pausing, zipping it. There's a difference you see. Ignoring things has no energy to it. It's passive. 'Masterful inactivity' has energy to it. It's a decision to wait; to pause; sometimes to just wait and see how things pan out. Other times just to breathe or to sleep on it.

Instead of responding to a flaming-arrow type of email or phone call, wait. We have to recognise an emergency and act on it, of course we do, but most of the time others' urgencies don't have to become *our* emergencies.

Often the person sending the message will either chase you up or – more often than not – call you to follow up or apologise. They often sort out the thing that they pounced on you to do and, if they don't, then you now have a choice. By waiting, pausing – even if it's just for 5 minutes – you also give yourself time to breathe. Take time to consider and you often take the energy, frustration and heat out of your own response.

When someone says something to you and you feel the 'arrrgghh' of frustration rise up or, often worse, the sarcastic voice which is so easy to use for your response, instead of going with it, wait. Pause. Sometimes you don't even *have* to comment and it's often far more powerful if you don't. You remember to breathe and you wait.

If you decide in that moment that you will adopt a bit of 'masterful inactivity' then you've made a decision as opposed to reacted.

Different. The other person will often be surprised and also their own heat may dissipate or they may re-think their decision or opinion. Either way, this is a powerful decision for you to make; to zip it. For you to choose how and if you respond, you're taking control when you could have been handing it over to the other person or to the situation. It's all part of you being understood as the person you want to be, as opposed to the one who's made to react. As someone who, by nature, used to be pretty fiery, I myself am still work-in-progress in this area.

Ideas for you to work with today:

- Be on the look-out for opportunities to adopt masterful inactivity. When you open an email, read it and then maybe put it into a file called 'Masterful Inactivity'. You can then keep an eye on when and how you respond, and it's easy to keep track of any you decide to file here.

- *Decide* if you're going to respond to someone or something. Notice *how* you decide. Are you thinking things through? Are you reacting to someone else's crisis or demand at the price of your own concentration, your own flow? You can often buy yourself some time by waiting, even if it's a second or two. Notice yourself and be more aware of how – and indeed if – you decide what to do next. You may just decide to zip it.

- Notice other people and how they react or respond. Some people you'll notice do 'zip it' and watch, wait and see. Watch *how* they do it and, depending on how you feel, ask them about it. As we've already explored together, when you notice something you like about someone and you comment on it, or ask him or her about it, they normally enjoy telling you about it and are pleased you've noticed. Interestingly too, they often don't know about it themselves so you give them the opportunity to *distinguish* what they're doing by asking them about it. That's how we learn, isn't it, being inquisitive? Asking, trying things out, trying things on for size, then making them our own.

Inspirations for you:

'There are times when silence has the loudest voice.'

Leroy Brownlow

'Silence is the most powerful scream.'

Unknown, but great!

'Saying nothing ... sometimes says the most.'

Emily Dickinson

Well, here we are.

We started at 'A is for Attitude' and here we are now together at 'Z is for Zip It' and every part of our journey is connected. I'm still on my journey too. Now it's over to you my friend to continue yours.

If I had known and been able to distinguish the principles in this book when I was in the day-to-day hubbub of my own corporate career, I would have made different decisions and had an easier time of things. My passion now, with my own business, is to pass on and share these powerful ways of connecting and engaging with people for my clients and for their success. Save the trial and error and the long-way-around and take the short cut, the proven way, the easier way to easily connect and be understood.

One of the trickiest lessons we learn in our lives is how to get along with people. How to be able to work with and alongside others, to persuade and engage people day-to-day to get things done and get our point across.

Writing this book after years of being asked questions like 'when are you going to write this stuff down Kay?' and 'where can I find out more about what you've just said?' that's my intention. For you to be able to get your own things done as you work with people to get your point across more quickly, more easily and more influentially. For you to save yourself loads of time, money and energy, three of our most precious resources – and for you to enjoy being understood.

'Every day you may make progress. Every step may be fruitful. Yet there will stretch out before you an ever-lengthening, ever-ascending, ever-improving path.

You know you will never get to the end of the journey. But this, so far from discouraging, only adds to the joy and glory of the climb.'

Winston Churchill

Works cited

Carnegie, Dale (1981) *How to Win Friends and Influence People*
London: Vermillion

Cialdini, Robert B (2007) *Influence: The Pyschology of Persuasion*
New York: HarperCollinsPublishers

Covey, Steven R (2004) *The 7 Habits of Highly Effective People*
London: Simon & Schuster

Goleman, Daniel (2006) *Emotional Intelligence*
New York: Bantam Dell

King, W J revisions and additions by James J Skakoon (2007)
The Unwritten Laws of Business
New York: Doubleday. This book was originally published in a
revised edition in 2001, by the American Society of Mechanical
Engineer under the title *The Unwritten Laws of Engineering*.

Pink, Daniel H (2005) *A Whole New Mind*
New York: The Berkeley Publishing Group

Pressfield, Steven (2007) *The War of Art*
New York: Grand Central Publishing

Free Additional Resources
from Kay White

Go to **www.wayforwardsolutions.com** and pick your *two free bonuses* to this book.

Firstly, your free supplement **Words that Work from A to Z**. The free downloadable document is the perfect add-on to this book.

Packed with lists of over 1,200 powerful, persuasive, inspiring and motivational words for you to use to boost your day-to-day conversations, your emails, reports, marketing and your presentations.

Set out from A to Z, the words will inspire and motivate you *and* make you more engaging and compelling to everyone around you, everywhere. They'll also make it easier for you as you practice the principles in this book.

Your second bonus is a powerful, free audio training '*How to Say No, Without Saying It*'.

Many people have contacted me telling me they really struggle with saying 'No' so I decided to set out *the exact words to say* and *the way to say them* in this free downloadable audio training so that it's *quick and straightforward for you* to be able to do it too. Be able to say 'No' and still come across as assertive and respectful at the same time.

Go to **www.wayforwardsolutions.com** and pick up your bonuses today and let's continue our conversation.

Kay White
Way Forward Solutions

Kay White discovered her talents at connecting and getting people into action whilst working both in Paris and in the City of London for more than twenty years.

Starting her career as a secretary and then working her way up to a Divisional Director, Kay was part of a successful, mainly male, fast-paced team of global insurance brokers. Learning (often by her own mistakes along the way) how to – *and crucially how not to* – get things done for, with and alongside people, Kay now shows her clients, all around the world, how to connect, build relationships and get their point of view more clearly, quickly and much more easily.

Proving time and again that by being understood and getting their messages across with more impact and influence, Kay's clients earn more, become more successful and feel more confident and comfortable as they go about their business, wherever they are. They often get on better with people at home too using the principles Kay shares.

Kay has developed Way Forward Solutions Ltd into a global mentoring and training company teaching professionals around the world how to be more visible, to be heard and be recognised and rewarded as they go about their work. All by understanding how and what they are communicating.

Offering live and virtual group training and mentorships Kay also works one-to-one with select VIP clients and this can either be in person or over the telephone and internet.

As a further resource *The A to Z of Being Understood*, Kay offers a 5-part audio teleseries called *Be Understood Now* and she walks you through more examples and stories from the 26 principles in this book. You'll find details of this plus further tools, tips, articles, case studies and additional resources when you visit **www.wayforwardsolutions.com**.

Lightning Source UK Ltd.
Milton Keynes UK
UKOW06f0415260216

269156UK00001B/98/P